AFRICAN AMERICAN TRAILBLAZERS

Ida B. Wells-Barnett

Suffragette and Social Activist

Naomi E. Jones

Cavendish Square

New York

Published in 2020 by Cavendish Square Publishing, LLC
243 5th Avenue, Suite 136, New York, NY 10016

Library of Congress Cataloging-in-Publication Data

Names: Jones, Naomi E.
Title: Ida B. Wells-Barnett : suffragette and social activist / Naomi E. Jones.
Description: New York : Cavendish Square, [2020] | Series: African American trailblazers |
Includes bibliographical references and index.
Identifiers: LCCN 2018047438 (print) | LCCN 2018047929 (ebook) | ISBN 9781502645623 (ebook) |
ISBN 9781502645616 (library bound) | ISBN 9781502645609 (pbk.)
Subjects: LCSH: Wells-Barnett, Ida B., 1862-1931--Juvenile literature. | African American women civil
rights workers--Biography--Juvenile literature. | Civil rights workers--United States--Biography--Juvenile
literature. | Journalists--United States--Biography--Juvenile literature. | Suffragists--United States--
Biography--Juvenile literature. | African Americans--Civil rights--History--Juvenile literature. | Lynching--
United States--History--Juvenile literature. | United States--Race relations--Juvenile literature.
Classification: LCC E185.97.W55 (ebook) | LCC E185.97.W55 J66 2020 (print) | DDC 323.092 [B] --dc23
LC record available at https://lccn.loc.gov/2018047438

Editorial Director: David McNamara
Editor: Kristen Susienka
Copy Editor: Alex Tessman
Associate Art Director: Alan Sliwinski
Designer: Joseph Parenteau
Production Coordinator: Karol Szymczuk
Photo Research: J8 Media

Printed in the United States of America

C O N T E N T S

INTRODUCTION

The Princess of the Press

I da B. Wells-Barnett grew up during the beginning of the Reconstruction period that followed the Civil War. This was a time of hope for newly freed slaves. As a child, Wells-Barnett saw her father vote for the first time, black men elected to government positions, educational opportunities for African Americans, and the passing of laws that forbade discrimination. However, before long she learned that racial violence would replace slavery, in the form of lynching.

Career and Opportunities

Wells-Barnett would have many professional opportunities throughout her life. She began a career at sixteen as a

This portrait shows Ida B. Wells-Barnett as a young woman in 1893.

teacher. Several events later would influence her transition into a lecturer, investigative journalist, and social justice advocate. Her lawsuit in 1884 against the Chesapeake, Ohio, and Southwestern Railroad for assault and discrimination led to the beginning of her journalist career. Wells-Barnett sent her first essay to a local newspaper in 1884, and within five years she had become the first woman owner and editor of a black newspaper in American history. Nicknamed the "Princess of the Press," she used her journalism career to fight prejudice and injustice through her writings, speeches, and protests. She fought lynching and worked to solve social issues such as poverty, poor housing, and inadequate schools.

Wells-Barnett met and befriended Frederick Douglass in 1892. They shared many goals, and he wrote letters of support for her and mentored her. She also worked with other civil rights leaders, including W. E. B. Du Bois. Although she helped many clubs and organizations that worked toward suffrage, civil rights, and urban reform, she never became a long-term member of any of them. Known for being blunt and outspoken, Wells-Barnett often ran into conflict with her fellow activists.

Spreading the Word

In the 1890s, she traveled across the East Coast and Great Britain giving talks on the racial injustices happening throughout the United States. Female lecturers were rare back then, but women were becoming increasingly active in reform movements, women's clubs, and fighting for suffrage.

After moving to Chicago, Wells-Barnett shifted her focus to women's suffrage and encouraged more women of color to get involved in politics and the suffrage movement. She had a great deal of faith in the power of voting, and before women

This collage of photographs features several famous African American leaders, including Ida B. Wells-Barnett (*bottom center*), Booker T. Washington (*left center*), and Frederick Douglass (*right*).

could vote, she worked to persuade men to vote for candidates who would fight lynching. She also urged women to vote once suffrage had been achieved.

Toward the end of her life, Wells-Barnett became one of the first African American women to run for public office in the United States, and the first female African American political activist to write an autobiography. Her contributions to civil rights would influence later twentieth-century activism.

GIBBON. CUSTAR. COMSTOCK. BABCOCK. MARTHALL. TAYLOR. SHERIDAN. RAWLINS. GRANT. MEADE. PARKER. FORSYTH. BOWERS. MERRITT. ORD.

The Room in the McLean House, at Appomattox C.H., in which GEN. LEE surrendered to GEN. GRANT.

CHAPTER ONE

Fighting for Equal Rights

The period known as Reconstruction began at the end of the Civil War. It lasted from 1865 to 1877. For a while, the newly freed slaves were able to attend school, hold public office, sit on juries, own businesses, and freely go into any public place. Many Northern reformers traveled south to assist the freedmen by providing them with food, assistance in integrating into society, and education. However, many of their newly acquired rights were taken away by the end of 1885. As violence, segregation, and disenfranchisement spread, African Americans were systematically denied the right to vote and condemned to second-class status.

This illustration depicts Robert E. Lee (*center left, seated*) surrendering to Ulysses S. Grant (*center right, seated*) at the end of the Civil War.

Reconstruction

Immediately after the Civil War and the end of slavery in the United States, many Southern states passed "black codes," which were intended to limit the personal freedom and rights of former slaves. They limited what jobs they could take, outlawed marriage between blacks and whites, imposed curfews, banned them from owning land or weapons, and banned them from juries and political meetings. To combat these racist laws, Congress passed a series of Reconstruction Acts during the 1860s. They established control over the former Confederate states until their new state governments were set up and gave former slaves the right to vote and run for office. These acts represented efforts to ensure former slaves would receive equal treatment under the law, and made provisions for public education and land redistribution. Under the Reconstruction Acts, blacks registered to vote and began attending school. For a short time, former Confederate leaders and military officers were restricted from voting and running for office.

The Fourteenth Amendment was ratified on July 28, 1868. It gave citizenship to former slaves and protected citizens from discrimination under state laws:

> All persons born or naturalized in the United States, and subject to the jurisdiction thereof, are citizens of the United States and the State wherein they reside. No State shall make or enforce any law which shall abridge the privileges or immunities of citizens of the United States; nor shall any State deprive any person of life, liberty, or property, without due process of law; nor deny to any person within its jurisdiction the equal protection of the laws.[1]

Each of the Confederate states was required to ratify this amendment as a condition of being allowed back into the Union.

Two years later, the Fifteenth Amendment was ratified. It gave African American men the right to vote: "The right of citizens of the United States to vote shall not be denied or abridged by the United States or by any State on account of race, color, or previous condition of servitude."[2]

That same year, the first African American congressmen were elected: Joseph H. Rainey of South Carolina to the House of Representatives and Hiram R. Revels of Mississippi to the Senate. Four years later, Blanche K. Bruce became the second African American to be elected to the Senate. A total of sixteen African Americans served in Congress during Reconstruction, and more served in state government positions and lower state offices, including postmasters and judges.

Congress passed a series of Enforcement Acts that dealt out federal penalties to states that attempted to interfere with the exercise of the rights guaranteed to African Americans under the Fourteenth Amendment. The Civil Rights Act of 1875 gave blacks the right to share public places with whites, stating that no public facility could legally refuse to admit any person on the basis of their race.

Working Conditions for Freedmen

Many former slaves remained in the South and wound up working for white landowners. As a result, a new economic system, called sharecropping, emerged. Now that they did not have slaves to work their entire plantation, landowners divided the land into smaller plots that could be farmed by single families. The sharecroppers worked the land and raised a crop, giving half of their harvest to the landowner in exchange for a house, supplies, and the right to live on the land. The

FREEDMEN'S AID AND EDUCATION

In the spring of 1865, Congress under President Abraham Lincoln established the Bureau of Freedmen, Refugees and Abandoned Lands, known simply as the Freedmen's Bureau, which was a government department meant to help both former slaves and white Southerners who had been left homeless by the Civil War. The Freedmen's Bureau distributed food and clothing to those in need and established schools and medical facilities.

Many former slaves were eager to become educated after emancipation. Very few freedmen could read and write, and many rushed to enroll after the Freedmen's Bureau began opening schools for blacks. In addition to the Freedmen's Bureau, thousands of teachers traveled from the North to join forces with Southern teachers to help educate former slaves. Some worked with the Freedmen's Bureau, and others came on their own. Many were women. The North had many organizations that worked to both assist and educate freedmen. In 1863, several of these organizations merged to become the United States Commission for the Relief of the National Freedman, later renamed the American Freedman's Aid Union. By 1870, this organization had opened more than 2,600 schools in the South.

Some of the first schools for blacks were established by the freedmen's agencies, and some by Northern churches. The Freedmen's Aid Society of the Methodist Church established many schools for newly freed slaves at the end of the Civil War. James Wells, the father of Ida B. Wells-Barnett, was actively involved with the Freedmen's Aid Society and a trustee of the school it established in 1866 in the family's hometown of Holly Springs: Shaw University, later renamed Rust College, which the Wells children attended.

landowners frequently exploited the workers, and many found themselves trapped in a system only marginally better than slavery. Although now free, they were frequently still oppressed. They now worked for pay, but typically received less than white workers and sometimes had difficulty collecting their wages—particularly from Southern planters who either couldn't or wouldn't pay them.

Some former slaves moved to the North but had difficulty finding jobs that were not either laborers or service people such as waiters, cooks, maids, and porters. Those who moved and took factory work often had to accept low pay and terrible working conditions due to lack of options. In contrast, self-employed blacks and those with specific skills tended to do well under Reconstruction, opening stores, hotels, cafés, and other businesses.

The End of Reconstruction

Reconstruction would end soon after the Civil Rights Act of 1875 was passed. Within two years of the ratification of the Fifteenth Amendment, the rights to vote and to hold office had been restored to most former Confederates. The results of the presidential election of 1876 were disputed, and an agreement was reached between the two parties in Congress to give Rutherford B. Hayes the victory. After Hayes was elected and took office in 1877, the Reconstruction period ended as the troops withdrew from the Southern states.

Soon thereafter, many white Southerners began working to rescind voting rights, political power, and social freedoms from African Americans. During the late 1870s, many African Americans began leaving the South. Between thirty thousand and fifty thousand of them moved west. Kansas was a popular destination. About twenty-five thousand people, known as

Exodusters, settled there. Many of them thrived, as they were treated better in Kansas than they were accustomed to in the South. Migration slowed in the 1880s, but beginning around the 1890s, blacks began leaving the South again in large numbers to escape discrimination.

Jim Crow

In 1875, the same year the Civil Rights Act of 1875 was passed giving blacks the right to sue for race discrimination in public places, Tennessee passed one of the first laws allowing business owners to refuse service or entrance to anyone they wanted. The system of segregation and discrimination rampant in the South was called "Jim Crow," named after a racist minstrel act. Jim Crow laws made it very difficult for African Americans to own property, and few could exercise their right to vote. The federal government had ceased enforcing the recent constitutional amendments.

Separate but (Not) Equal

In October 1883, the Supreme Court ruled the Civil Rights Act of 1875 unconstitutional, claiming it violated states' rights and that civil rights should be decided by the individual states, rather than the federal government. This enabled states to legalize forced segregation. To be ruled unconstitutional, a law had to explicitly declare that it was put in place to deny a person access to public facilities based on race alone.

In 1890, the state of Louisiana passed a law that mandated separate train cars for blacks and whites. Homer Plessy, a man who was one-eighth black, was arrested for traveling in the whites-only car. He took his case to the Supreme Court, where his attorney argued that the state law violated the Fourteenth

This classroom is a small blacks-only schoolhouse, the Anthoston Colored School in Kentucky. This photo was taken in 1916, during a wave of segregation in the United States.

Amendment. However, on May 18, 1896, the Supreme Court ruled in *Plessy v. Ferguson* that laws mandating segregation were constitutional as long as both races were provided with equal options. "Separate but equal" public services were now legal under the Fourteenth Amendment. In reality, businesses only had to provide the service for both races and claim that they were equal provisions. Rarely if ever were such provisions actually equal.

Segregation was occurring everywhere, including in the federal government. There were segregated schools, separate seating on public transportation and in theaters and restaurants, separate public restrooms and water fountains, even segregation in cemeteries. Under the guise of "separate but equal," the accommodations for blacks were usually inferior to those provided to whites.

Violence and Disenfranchisement

Many African Americans continued exercising their right to vote through the early 1880s, although this became dangerous for them after the departure of the army due to the threat of violence. Since blacks outnumbered whites in many Southern states, white supremacists were concerned about blacks gaining political power and began a campaign of disenfranchisement tactics to maintain their control. After Reconstruction, they increased their attempts to suppress black political and economic freedom with mob violence. Lynching became a common practice. Over 1,400 African Americans were lynched in the United States between 1890 and 1903. In 1892, there were over 250, more than in any other year. Victims were often tortured and mutilated before being murdered.

Lynching was community sanctioned and often publicized in advance as it was, horrifyingly enough, a form of entertainment in certain communities. Few perpetrators were ever punished, despite being known. They claimed that the victims had been lynched as punishment for crimes, particularly murder and rape, but many lynch victims were never formally accused of these crimes, and charges of rape were frequently untrue. However, the guilt of the victims for whatever crimes they were accused of was never questioned by the community. Many victims were only declared to have committed crimes after they had already been murdered. In reality, African Americans were lynched for offenses such as insulting a white man, trying to get a job viewed as being above their station, or trying to exercise their right to vote.

The Fourteenth and Fifteenth Amendments did not outlaw literacy tests or poll taxes, provided that qualifications for voting did not state that they explicitly were directed at African Americans. They did not guarantee that African Americans could hold office, nor did they prevent the exclusion of them from voting based on a grandfather clause or property requirement.

Many tactics were used in an attempt to prevent African Americans from voting. By 1910, all the Southern states had instituted a poll tax, usually of one or two dollars, which was the equivalent of several days' pay for a laborer. Frequently, laws requiring a literacy test would only be applied in districts with a large black population, and poll workers would assist illiterate whites, while black voters would be required to fill out applications perfectly with no assistance. Overly complicated ballot boxes making it nearly impossible to get the ballot into the correct slot and ballot boxes with false bottoms were used. Often, polling places in areas with a large number of black voters would be closed illegally during elections or open at odd hours. A grandfather clause waived other voting requirements for those individuals who had voted before or whose grandfather had voted, which left out former slaves.

Despite these disenfranchisement attempts, many African Americans persisted in exercising their right to vote. As writer and historian Lawrence Goldstone wrote, "after a century of being denied, even these machinations, widespread as they were, could not be counted on to suppress African-Americans' will to vote. Blacks continued to endure abuse and risk bodily harm in order to try to cast ballots."[3]

The Progressive Era

The Progressive Era, lasting from the 1890s to the 1920s, was a period of reform in several areas of American life, including economic, social, and political reforms. Issues at stake included prohibition of alcohol, labor regulations such as sweatshop reform and the abolishment of child labor, regulation of trusts, and women's suffrage. Most of the reformers were in cities and members of the college-educated middle class. Many reformers were women, both individually and through women's organizations, who worked primarily for suffrage and other equality issues, social reforms, improvements to schools, child labor regulations, and prohibition. Reformers also fought government corruption and attempted to regulate business and improve working conditions.

During this era, investigative journalists known as muckrakers worked to expose society's evils, such as corruption in government and business, child labor, and lynching. As a result, laws were passed to restrict child labor, improve factory conditions, and regulate industries such as the railroads and the meat-packing industry. Public health campaigns resulted in the reduction of disease and child mortality. Attempts were made by reformers to improve the conditions of housing, public schools, and employment.

Settlement Houses

The settlement house movement was a key part of the Progressive Era beginning in the late nineteenth century. A settlement house was a building in which reformers would live and provide community services, particularly to poor and immigrant urban populations. It represented a more hands-on approach to charitable work. This was a reform movement that took place in cities across the United States, with the intent of providing a never-before-seen service to the poor. The movement had actually begun in Britain during the 1880s, with the very first settlement house, Toynbee Hall, being founded in London in 1884. American reformers Jane Addams and Ellen Gates Starr had visited Toynbee Hall and were inspired to open the first settlement house in the United States. Hull House was founded in Chicago in 1889. It had public baths, housing for working women, and Chicago's first kindergarten, as well as an art gallery and theater that assisted with cultural assimilation for immigrants. By 1910, there were more than four hundred

THE HULL HOUSE, CHICAGO

This postcard depicts the Hull House, Chicago's first settlement house, founded by Jane Addams and Ellen Gates Starr in 1889. Hull House provided services for Chicago's poor and immigrant populations.

settlement houses in the United States, with women serving as the majority of settlement workers.

In many major cities, large numbers of immigrants lived in poverty in crowded slums. Settlement houses served to help them assimilate into American society by giving them the tools they needed to get out of poverty and overcome isolation. Particularly during periods of increased immigration, settlement workers assisted new arrivals and taught them American values and customs to enable their assimilation. They also worked to assist industrial workers and their families.

Settlement houses were also used by reformers to gather data about poor populations in order to better propose legislation to improve their conditions. Settlement workers often lived among the people they helped, in order to better understand how the poor and immigrant populations lived and what reforms would best assist them. They provided employment counseling, child care, education for both children and adults, and health services.

Many settlement houses were founded by women, usually of the middle class. The level of female leadership in this reform movement was unprecedented. However, most settlement house founders were white and tended to ignore the needs of the African American poor, even in light of the mass migration of Southern blacks to Northern cities that was taking place during this time. Between 1915 and 1925, a large number of African Americans migrated to the North, due to a combination of racial prejudice and Jim Crow laws in the South and the high demand for workers in factories and increased industrial work in cities. For this reason, churches and women's clubs in black communities did their own settlement movement work for poor African American migrants.

After 1917, the United States entered World War I, which led to a decrease in immigration and less public or government concern over urban poverty. This resulted in a decline in the settlement house movement during the 1920s. By the 1930s, federal social welfare programs under the New Deal had been initiated, replacing the work that settlement houses had been doing.

Votes for Women

Many women joined the antislavery movement, which began in the 1830s, but they frequently were discriminated against by male activists within the movement, who refused to accept the idea of women involving themselves in political action. In 1840, abolitionist Lucretia Mott and several other women were denied entrance to a London antislavery convention. Mott and Elizabeth Cady Stanton, another abolitionist, decided to start fighting for women's rights in addition to their cause of abolishing slavery. Mott and Stanton, along with other feminists, organized the first Women's Rights Convention in Seneca Falls, New York, in July 1848. Three hundred people attended, including forty men. At the convention, a Declaration of Sentiments, modeled after the Declaration of Independence, was drafted in which the women declared their "inalienable rights" as citizens.[4]

When the Civil War started, many women's rights advocates, including Stanton and Susan B. Anthony, put aside their cause to focus on abolishing slavery. Feminists like Stanton and Anthony were instrumental in helping gain approval for the Thirteenth Amendment, which ended slavery in the United States. After the end of the Civil War, Anthony and others insisted that the Fourteenth Amendment should grant rights to women in addition to African American men. However, many male abolitionist leaders, including Frederick Douglass, told them to wait, as they felt including women's rights would make it more difficult to get the amendment to pass Congress.

Women's rights activists split after the Civil War over the issue of whether or not they should fight to ensure that voting rights for women were included in the Fifteenth Amendment, which granted the vote to African American men. In 1869, two organizations emerged. Susan B. Anthony and Elizabeth Cady Stanton formed the National Woman Suffrage Association in New York, which wanted to immediately begin the push for women's suffrage. This organization worked on other social issues as well, and typically did not allow male involvement. The American Woman Suffrage Association, formed by former abolitionist Lucy Stone in Boston, wanted to first fight to ensure the vote for African American men, and focused solely on suffrage issues. They welcomed men into their ranks and worked on gaining women's suffrage on a state by state basis.

As the economy of the United States changed during the mid-1880s with the opening of factories, women began taking employment outside of the home. Although most went into teaching and nursing, they began to work in businesses and factories as well, though they were never paid as much as men. Any attempt by women to join an occupation traditionally held by men was typically resisted and ridiculed, as the common belief of the time was that men and women had different roles, and that women belonged in the home. Gender bias and belief in "traditional" gender roles were common reasons why many people opposed women's suffrage as well. Some argued that the involvement of women in politics would degrade family values, or that women were too emotional to get involved in political issues. Some women even opposed suffrage, arguing in favor of traditional gender roles and insisting that getting involved in politics would be improper. Others who opposed women voting were large business owners who were afraid that women would vote to limit work hours and ban child labor, as well as liquor manufacturers and saloon owners, who feared that women would vote to ban alcohol. In fact, the Nineteenth Amendment granting women suffrage was not ratified until a year after the institution of prohibition.

In 1878, at the urging of Elizabeth Cady Stanton, Senator A.A. Sargent of California introduced an amendment in Congress to grant suffrage to women. The "Susan B. Anthony Amendment," as it was called, did not pass, but would be reintroduced almost every year for the next forty years.

In the meantime, several Western states began giving women the right to vote. The first was Wyoming, which, although only a territory in 1869 when it granted women suffrage, became a state in 1890. By 1896, women could also vote in Colorado, Idaho, and Utah. Within twenty years, this list had grown to eleven states, including Arizona, California, Kansas, Montana, Nevada, Oregon, and Washington.

The two competing suffrage organizations, the National Woman Suffrage Association and the American Woman Suffrage Association, merged in 1890 and became the National American Woman Suffrage Association (NAWSA). In 1915, former schoolteacher Carrie Chapman Catt became head of the organization. Born in Iowa, she had graduated valedictorian and the only woman in her class from Iowa State College. Catt developed a strategy that involved simultaneously working toward an amendment to the US Constitution and individual state laws to allow women suffrage.

Other suffragists, however, led by Alice Paul, the leader of the National Woman's Party, preferred more powerful tactics such as picketing, holding marches, and outdoor rallies. In

Women picket the White House as part of the 1917 protests for suffrage. The picketing and subsequent arrests forced President Wilson to act and support the Nineteenth Amendment, which gave women the right to vote.

January 1917, Paul and her faction began picketing the White House to convince President Woodrow Wilson to support the proposed Anthony Amendment giving women the right to vote. They did this throughout the year, marching in front of the White House with banners and risking physical attacks. Between June and November, 218 protesters were arrested for obstructing sidewalk traffic. On August 28, ten suffragists,

including Paul herself, were arrested. They went on a hunger strike in jail and had to be force-fed.

Because of the picketing and arrests, suffragists could no longer be ignored by the administration. In January 1918, President Wilson succumbed to pressure from the publicity of the force-feeding of women protestors and chose to support the women's suffrage amendment. The bill passed Congress in the summer of 1919, and was ratified as the Nineteenth Amendment on August 18, 1920.

CHAPTER TWO

A Personal History of Ida B. Wells–Barnett

I da Bell Wells (who later became Ida B. Wells–Barnett after she married in 1895) was born a slave on July 16, 1862, in Holly Springs, Mississippi, a town that changed hands many times during the Civil War. She was the first of eight children born to James Wells and Elizabeth Warrenton. James Wells was the only son of his master and had been sent to Holly Springs at eighteen to become an apprentice to Spires Bolling, a carpenter. Elizabeth was Bolling's cook. She was born into slavery in Virginia and eventually sold into Mississippi.

Parental Influence

The Civil War was over by Wells–Barnett's third birthday, and her parents, who had married as slaves, married

This photograph shows the downtown area of modern-day Holly Springs, Mississippi.

again as free people, since their marriage as slaves had not been legally recognized. They continued to work for Bolling for wages until 1867, which was the first year that freedmen could vote under the Reconstruction Act. James Wells had refused to vote for the candidate Bolling supported, and returned from the polls to find his home and workshop on his employer's property locked. He immediately went into town, rented another house, bought new carpentry tools, and established his own carpentry business.

Both Wells-Barnett's parents did well during Reconstruction due to their skills. James had a great deal of work rebuilding homes and other buildings that had been destroyed during the war. In 1870, he purchased a lot and built a new house for the family.

Both James and Elizabeth saw great value in education. Once slavery ended, they ensured that their children attended school. Elizabeth attended as well: a religious woman, she wanted to learn how to read the Bible.

Wells-Barnett was very close to her father, who encouraged her intellectually. James Wells was politically active, a Master Mason, and a leader in the African American community of Holly Springs. From an early age, Wells-Barnett's introduction to politics was through her father, reading newspapers aloud to him and his friends and listening to their discussions. He voted and attended political meetings.

Head of the Household

In 1878, Wells-Barnett was out of town visiting her grandmother when she received word that her parents and youngest brother had died in the yellow fever epidemic that was sweeping the South. She was desperate to return home; however, she was urged not to. Her grandmother expressly forbade her from going home until she received a letter from Dr. D. H. Gray, who had tended them at the end of their lives, asking Wells-Barnett to return immediately to sort out her parents' affairs. No passenger trains were running due to the epidemic, so she had to travel on board a freight train. She was told by the conductor that she was making a mistake.

Wells-Barnett was one of eight. One brother, Eddie, had died as a young child, and the baby, Stanley, was killed in the outbreak along with their parents. Remaining were her three sisters, Eugenia, Annie, and Lily, and her two brothers, James and George. Her father's fellow Masons met and decided to split up the children, each taking in one or two and sending Eugenia, who was physically disabled, to the poorhouse.

Wells-Barnett approached the Masons to intervene. She insisted that since the family owned their house and their parents had left them a sum of money in the care of Dr. Gray, she would take care of her younger siblings in order to keep the family together. All she asked was that the Masons help her to find work so that she could support everyone. They agreed, and advised her to seek a teaching job. Wells-Barnett passed the teacher's exam and, at the age of sixteen, took a job at a school in rural Mississippi, a few miles from Holly Springs.

Wells-Barnett took care of her siblings on her own for a short time, and then ran into difficulty. She had met Dr. Gray in town to get her father's money, which the doctor had locked in a safe. Townspeople had witnessed her meeting Dr. Gray, and some had started a rumor that Wells-Barnett had been seen asking white men for money. To preserve her reputation, her grandmother came to stay with the children.

After her grandmother had a stroke and had to move back home, a friend of Wells-Barnett's mother came to look after the

A MARITAL AND POLITICAL PARTNERSHIP

When Ida Wells married Ferdinand Barnett, an ambitious lawyer and a widower with two sons, on June 27, 1895, the pair formed a partnership based not only on love but on mutual beliefs and complementary career goals. They had gotten to know each other while collaborating on a pamphlet at the World's Columbian Exposition in Chicago, and fully supported each other's political fights. They shared political views, although Barnett was less combative about them than his wife.

Barnett was born free, as his father had purchased both his and his wife's freedom. He was educated in Canada and later attended Chicago College of Law, which became Northwestern University Law School. Like Wells, he worked as a teacher before becoming a journalist. In 1878, at the age of twenty-six, Barnett founded the *Conservator*, the first black weekly newspaper in Chicago, and began working as its publisher. He had been an activist throughout the 1870s, once giving a speech at a convention called "Race Unity: Its Importance, Necessity, Causes Which Retard Its Development." The *Conservator* published editorials denouncing lynching, and Barnett had helped found the Illinois Anti-Lynching League. As an attorney, Barnett did a great deal of pro bono, or free-of-charge, work defending African American men who were arrested.

In 1896, Barnett became the first African American assistant state's attorney, a position he held for fifteen years. He became an expert on habeas corpus and extradition, developed procedures for juvenile court, and prosecuted antitrust violations against large corporations. In this position, he knew quickly of racial injustice occurring within the state of Illinois. When his job prevented him from doing anything about it, Ida went in his place. He was nominated for a municipal judgeship in 1906, and ran for the position that November. At the first count of the votes he won, but following a supposed recount, the election officials reversed the results.

Their marriage was not traditional for the time, as each had sought not only a spouse but also a career partner. The couple helped and supported each other's work, and often worked together to fight injustice. They were both interested in prisoners' rights, and worked with the Board of Pardons, testifying together on behalf of prisoners whom they believed were innocent.

children while Wells-Barnett was at work. In 1881, her aunt Fannie Butler, her father's sister, invited the family to live with her in Memphis, Tennessee. Wells-Barnett's brothers, James and George, had recently left home to become carpenters and her sister Eugenia had moved in with another aunt, so it was only Ida, Annie, and Lily who made the move to Memphis once Wells-Barnett had gotten a teaching job in the city.

Battling the Railroad

Segregation on railroads was common in the post-Reconstruction South. Most trains had a first-class "ladies" car and a colored car, which the railroad insisted was also a first-class car for the purposes of maintaining the guise of "separate but equal" accommodations. Although the cars cost the same, they were, in fact, far from equal. There were rules in place against swearing, drinking, and smoking in the first-class cars, but the conductors did not enforce these rules in the first-class colored car. It was frequently used by white men as a lounge for smoking and drinking, and made indistinguishable from the second-class cars. African American men and women had to use the same bathroom on the train, whereas white men and women had separate facilities. Passengers in the colored car often had to share the space with train personnel, there were often few seats, and it tended to be crowded.

Wells-Barnett took the train to and from her teaching job, and always bought a first-class train ticket for the ladies' car since the colored/smoker car was noisy, hot, and sooty from being closer to the engine. The ladies' car was smoke-free, more comfortable, and safer for a woman traveling alone. For two years she had few problems. However, on September 15, 1883, this changed. Wells-Barnett was seated in the ladies' car on the train from Memphis and the conductor refused to take her ticket, telling her to move to the smoking car. When she refused, he grabbed her arm to pull her out of her seat, and she bit him on the hand. With the assistance of three other men, the conductor pushed her out of the train car at the next station. Upon her return home, she filed a lawsuit against the railroad. In the case of *Wells vs. Chesapeake, Ohio & Southwestern Railroad*, Judge James O. Pierce, a former Union soldier, ruled in her favor, awarding her $500 (about $13,000 in 2018) in damages.

Wells-Barnett's victory was sadly short lived. The railroad filed an appeal in the Tennessee State Supreme Court, and on April 11, 1887, Wells-Barnett learned that the court had reversed the initial decision. She was ordered to pay over $200 (about $5,300 in 2018) in court costs. Heartbroken at this turn of events, she wrote in her diary:

> The Supreme Court reversed the decision of the lower court in my behalf … four of them cast their personal prejudices in the scale of justice and decided in face of all evidence to the contrary that the smoking car was a first class coach for colored people as provided for by that statute that calls for separate coaches but first class, for the races. I felt so disappointed, because I had hoped such great things from my suit for my people generally. I have firmly believed all along that the law was on our side and would, when we appealed to it, give us justice. I feel shorn of that belief and utterly discouraged.[1]

The Birth of Iola

During the 1880s, black lyceums and literary societies were being established across the country. This included the

Memphis Lyceum, established by black teachers in 1883. They met weekly and held debates, readings, music performances, and recitations. Wells-Barnett joined the lyceum shortly after moving to Memphis, making her first public performance in the spring of 1885. In addition to the reading of essays and poetry, the Memphis Lyceum members published a journal, the *Evening Star*, which they read aloud during meetings.

Wells-Barnett was elected editor of the *Evening Star* in 1886 after the existing editor left town. Her talents led to an increase in attendance at lyceum meetings, as well as increased attention to her work as a journalist. Her work began to be featured in an increasing number of publications, and she was a regular correspondent for *The American Baptist Magazine*.

She was soon invited to write for a black church paper, *The Living Way*. Wells-Barnett wrote an article about her experience with her lawsuit for the paper, following which she began to write a weekly column using the pen name "Iola." Wells-Barnett initially received little or no payment for her writing, but by 1886, her reports on black life in Tennessee were published in multiple newspapers.

In July 1886, the National Education Association held a meeting in Topeka, Kansas, which Wells-Barnett and other Memphis teachers decided to attend. Accompanied by her colleagues, Wells-Barnett took a train to Topeka, and afterward continued out West, through Colorado, Utah, and California. She had been given assignments from the *Living Way* to report on famous sites and landmarks at various stops along the way, including Denver, Salt Lake City, and San Francisco, and met a number of editors, women's club members, and prominent African Americans. Her final destination was Visalia, California, where her aunt Fannie had recently moved along with Wells-Barnett's sisters.

Wells-Barnett did not intend to remain long in Visalia. She only wanted to go to see her sisters and convince her aunt, who wanted her to settle in Visalia as well, that she should remain living in Memphis. However, upon arrival, Wells-Barnett succumbed to her aunt's wishes and agreed to stay a while to help raise her sisters and to teach in Visalia's school for African American children. When her aunt begged her to stay for the year to help her with the children, Wells-Barnett reluctantly sold her return train ticket. She became unhappy in Visalia, complaining in her diary of the heat and how dull she found the small town.

Desperate to leave Visalia, Wells-Barnett reached out to an acquaintance in Memphis. Robert Church had been born a slave and was now a wealthy property owner. She asked him if he would loan her $150 (about $4,000 in 2018) to return to Memphis, on the condition that she was reelected to teach in the city. He agreed to help her and, against her aunt's wishes, she was able to return. She had been in Visalia for about a month and a half, and had only taught there for four days. Her sister Annie wanted to stay in California, so Wells-Barnett only took Lily back with her to Memphis.

By 1889, Wells-Barnett had become well known as a skilled and passionate journalist, earning the nickname "The Princess of the Press." This year marked a crucial phase of her career. Believing she would earn more as a journalist if she published her own work, Wells-Barnett accepted the invitation of pastor Taylor Nightingale to become the editor of the *Memphis Free Speech and Headlight*, which was published from the basement of the Beale Street Church. Her acceptance of the job was conditional on her being made an equal partner with Nightingale and J. L. Fleming, the paper's business manager. Wells-Barnett bought a one-third interest in the paper and

343.2 W

PRICE 25 CENTS.

A RED RECORD.

Tabulated Statistics and Alleged Causes of

Lynchings in the United States,

1892-1893-1894.

Respectfully submitted to the Nineteenth Century
civilization in "the Land of the Free and
the Home of the Brave."

BY
MISS IDA B. WELLS,
128 Clark Street,
CHICAGO.

DONOHUE & HENNEBERRY, PRINTERS, BINDERS AND ENGRAVERS, CHICAGO

This is the front cover of Wells-Barnett's second pamphlet, *A Red Record*, published in 1895. In it, she detailed lynching statistics and exposed racism and lies as the motives of the murderers.

began her job as editor. The paper was successful under her leadership, and she soon increased the number of subscriptions. Illiteracy among African American adults at this time was high. Many who could not read would still purchase newspapers for public reading by a literate friend or relative. Wells-Barnett came up with the idea of printing the *Free Speech* on pink paper to ensure that illiterate people would be able to identify it.

In 1891, she wrote an editorial protesting the conditions of segregated schools in Memphis, which included criticism of the inadequate facilities and unfit teachers provided for black schools. She lost her teaching job as a result, but found a new way to support herself. She began traveling to sell subscriptions to the *Free Speech*, soon making more money than she had made as a teacher. In addition, she managed to increase circulation of the newspaper from less than 1,500 subscribers to 4,000 over the course of nine months.

Exiled from Memphis

The following year, the course of Wells-Barnett's life changed dramatically due to a tragic event. Her friend Thomas Moss and his business partners, Will Stewart and Calvin McDowell, were lynched in March 1892 after a dispute between the grocery store they owned and the white-owned store nearby.

The rivalry between the stores had escalated to the point where a fight between two boys over a game of marbles erupted into a larger fight between whites and blacks. The People's Grocery had been established in 1889 by the three men and had been successful, to the irritation of W.H. Barrett, the owner of the competing store. Barrett spread a rumor that a white mob was coming to attack the People's Grocery, but instead he led a group of deputies to the store one night. Stewart and

McDowell had amassed a group of armed men to defend their property, anticipating the attack. They fired on the white men in self-defense, not realizing there were police officers among them. All three store owners—despite the fact that Moss had not been present but had been at home that night—were arrested and imprisoned. After three days in jail, a mob of seventy-five masked men surrounded the jail, dragged the three men out, and shot them to death. There was no punishment for the murderers.

Wells-Barnett heard about the lynching while she was out of town on newspaper business. Naturally, as a close friend of Moss, she was distraught. She mourned in her autobiography:

> Everybody in town knew and loved Tommie. An exemplary young man, he was married and the father of one little girl, Maurine, whose godmother I was. He and his wife Betty were the best friends I had in town. And he believed, with me, that we should defend the cause of right and fight wrong wherever we saw it.[2]

The lynching of Thomas Moss and his associates changed her life. She later wrote in her autobiography: "This is what opened my eyes to what lynching really was. An excuse to get rid of Negroes who were acquiring wealth and property and thus keep the race terrorized."[3]

In the first editorial she wrote after the murders, after it became clear that local authorities would make no attempt to punish the killers, who were known, Wells-Barnett urged African Americans to leave Memphis. She also developed an interest in the investigation and reporting of lynchings, becoming one of the first journalists to research and gather

4E   106

PEOPLE'S GROCERY

Thomas Moss, Calvin McDowell, and Will Stewart, all African-Americans and co-owners of People's Grocery (located at this site), were arrested in connection with a distrubance near their store. Rather than being brought to trial, they were lynched on March 9, 1892. Moss' dying words were, "Tell my people to go west -- there is no justice for them here." This lynching prompted Ida B. Wells, editor of *Memphis Free Speech* to begin her anti-lynching campaign in this country and abroad.

TENNESSEE HISTORICAL COMMISSION

This marker stands at the corner of Walker Avenue and Mississippi Boulevard in Memphis, Tennessee. It commemorates the former site of the People's Grocery and the lynching of Thomas Moss, Calvin McDowell, and Will Stewart.

evidence about the true causes of lynching. In particular, she demonstrated that while most lynchings were claimed to be punishment for crimes, in reality they were actually attempts by whites to keep African Americans subservient.

On May 21, 1892, Wells-Barnett published another editorial in response to the murder of Moss, this time on the findings from her lynching investigations. This sparked a furious reaction from many whites in Memphis. On May 26, a mob broke into the office of the *Free Speech* and destroyed it. No one was in the office at the time, and a note was left threatening to kill anyone trying to publish the paper again.

Wells-Barnett herself was on her way to New York City when this occurred. The editor of the prominent African American newspaper the *New York Age*, T. Thomas Fortune, met her at the train station and told her about the threats to her life being made if she returned to Memphis. Wells-Barnett also received telegrams from friends saying that her home was being watched, and men were asking after her whereabouts and watching the train station for her return. Many were calling for her to be hanged.

It was clear to Wells-Barnett that she could not return home to Memphis. She accepted a one-quarter interest in the *New York Age* in exchange for her *Free Speech* subscription list, became a weekly contributor to the paper, and found a place to live in New York. With the *New York Age*, she wrote more anti-lynching editorials as well as articles comparing race relations in the North and the South.

Shortly after she had moved to New York City, the friends she had made there decided to plan an event in her honor. They formed the Ida B. Wells Testimonial Reception Committee, which organized the event at Lyric Hall on October 5, 1892. Wells-Barnett was given $500 to go toward starting her own paper, and gave an emotional speech about the tragic events in Memphis which had led to her exile. Although she had learned public speaking during her time in the lyceum in Memphis, this was her first time delivering an "honest-to-goodness address."[4]

The Lyric Hall reception was the beginning of two things: the club movement for black women, and Wells-Barnett's public speaking career. Following the event, the planners

Here is an early photograph of Wells-Barnett as a young journalist. It was taken around the time of her exile from Memphis and the beginning of her career as a lecturer.

turned the New York committee into the Women's Loyal Union, New York City's first African American women's club. Women from Boston who had attended returned home and formed the Woman's Era Club, a similar organization. These clubs served as both social gatherings and a means of social and political reform. Soon thereafter, Wells-Barnett received invitations to speak in New York City, Boston, Philadelphia, and Washington, DC. She gave speeches throughout the Northeast and became quite a popular speaker, even traveling to Great Britain for speaking tours.

After returning from a trip to England in 1893, Wells-Barnett proceeded to Chicago for the World's Columbian Exposition, which would propel her into the next phase of her life.

Her Life in Chicago

After the exposition, Wells-Barnett decided to stay in Chicago instead of returning to New York. She had accepted a job with the *Chicago Conservator*, the oldest black newspaper in the city, and organized the first black women's club in Illinois, which the members had named after her.

She had begun a relationship with Ferdinand Barnett, a widowed lawyer and the editor of the *Conservator*, whom she had met through a mutual friend and gotten to know at the exposition. Barnett had two sons from his previous marriage and had lost his wife in 1888 to a heart attack. He was ten years older than Wells, but the two shared a passion for the same political issues. The couple married on June 27, 1895, after three postponements due to Wells's out-of-town speaking engagements. She chose to hyphenate her name—an unusual choice for the time—in order to keep the identity with which

FERDINAND L. BARNETT,
Assistant State's Attorney of the State of Illinois.

This photograph of Ferdinand L. Barnett was taken during his tenure as assistant state's attorney. Barnett was also the editor of the *Chicago Conservator* before turning the position over to his wife.

she had begun her career, becoming Ida B. Wells-Barnett. After the wedding, she took over the editorship of the *Conservator*.

The couple's first son, Charles, was born on March 25, 1896. Initially unwilling to give up her work and speaking engagements, Wells-Barnett brought baby Charles everywhere with her, to meetings and other activities. However, soon Wells-Barnett was, in her own words as written in her autobiography, "thoroughly convinced by this time that the duties of wife and mother were a profession in themselves and it was hopeless to expect to carry on public work."[5] She announced her retirement in 1897 after the birth of her second son, Herman, giving up her position as editor of the *Conservator* and selling the paper, with the intention of giving up her career in order to focus on raising her children. The divestment of the *Conservator* may also have been related to her husband's appointment as assistant state's attorney for Cook County. Her retirement, however, only lasted for five months, after which she began traveling for meetings and speaking engagements once more, this time bringing baby Herman along.

Two daughters followed, Ida in 1901 and Alfreda in 1904. Alfreda would eventually go on to finish, edit, and posthumously publish her mother's autobiography, *Crusade for Justice*.

Clubs and Organizations

Wells-Barnett was involved in the Niagara Movement with W. E. B. Du Bois in 1906, and was one of the founding members of the movement's successor organization, the National Association for the Advancement of Colored People (NAACP), in 1909. The NAACP grew quickly, with fifty branches by 1914 and four hundred by 1920. The organization used legal action to fight Jim Crow injustice. Wells-Barnett

This image shows the members of the Niagara Movement, including W. E. B. Du Bois (*front, seated, left*), taken in Boston, Massachusetts, in 1907. The Niagara Movement would be succeeded by the NAACP, which grew quickly as it fought segregation.

eventually left the NAACP due to conflict with its leadership, and skepticism about its ability to fight lynching.

In 1910, Wells-Barnett and her husband founded the Negro Fellowship League, an organization designed to help impoverished African American migrants. The Negro Fellowship League consisted of a lodging house, an employment agency, and a reading room, among other settlement house services. Three years later, she founded the Alpha Suffrage Club, an organization devoted to rallying African American women to work for women's suffrage.

Her Final Years

Wells-Barnett was a member of a committee that approached President Wilson in 1915 and asked him to work on abolishing segregation and other forms of racial discrimination. In 1918, she was asked to attend the Versailles Peace Conference in Paris at the end of World War I, although the United States government would deny her a passport because of her reputation as a radical. She was forced by financial difficulties to close the Negro Fellowship League in 1920. Soon after, she had to have surgery after being diagnosed with gallstones, and was bedridden for about a year afterward.

In 1930, Wells-Barnett gathered signatures to oppose the US occupation of Haiti, finishing with eighty-five signatures. Later that year, unsatisfied with the job that Illinois legislators were doing and concerned about unemployment levels in the black neighborhoods of Chicago, she ran for election to the Illinois state senate. She lost the election, but was one of the first African American women to run for public office in the United States. She was in poor health by this point in her life, and died of kidney disease on March 25, 1931.

CHAPTER THREE

Allies and Opponents

While she was not always well-liked due to her outspoken nature, Wells-Barnett collaborated with and even befriended several other leading figures in both the civil rights and women's suffrage movements on multiple occasions. She and her contemporaries were often, although not always, able to put aside their differences for the sake of their common goals.

Susan B. Anthony

Susan B. Anthony was born in Adams, Massachusetts, on February 15, 1820, one of eight children. As a child she was denied math education because she was a girl, so her

Women's suffrage activist Susan B. Anthony worked hard to secure the vote for women.

father set up a home school program for her and her sisters. Her father, Daniel Anthony, an abolitionist, was a major influence on her life and work. He worked with Frederick Douglass and a number of other abolitionist leaders. Anthony began teaching at the age of fifteen, and because of this experience, she later fought for equal pay for female teachers. At sixteen, she was collecting antislavery ballots and participating in abolitionist meetings with her father. The family moved to Rochester, New York, in 1845, and she attended the Woman's Rights Convention in Seneca Falls in 1848.

Anthony was a leader in the Rochester branch of the Daughters of Temperance, an organization working for stronger liquor laws. Although she did not consider herself to be a good public speaker, she was passionate about several causes and attended multiple meetings to give talks on temperance, abolition, and women's suffrage. In 1851, when she was met with male hostility to her temperance work, she became convinced that women needed to have the right to vote and to speak in public in order to accomplish anything. She met feminist Elizabeth Cady Stanton in 1851 at a temperance meeting in Seneca Falls, and the pair began traveling together to give talks about women's equality.

Anthony campaigned door-to-door, in government, and in meetings for the abolition of slavery and for women's rights. In 1854, she collected ten thousand signatures on a petition to support women's suffrage and property rights for married women. At this time in New York, the property and wages of a married woman legally belonged to a woman's husband. This changed in 1860 due to Anthony's work. With the enactment of the New York State Married Women's Property and Guardianship Law, married women gained control over their earnings and the right to guardianship over their children.

In 1856, Anthony joined the American Anti-Slavery Society of New York. She put the fight for women's rights aside in 1861 at the beginning of the Civil War, and instead organized the Women's National Loyal League to push for passage of the Thirteenth Amendment, which would abolish slavery. She spoke often about African American rights, having been influenced by her father's and then her own friendship with Frederick Douglass. In 1865, she tried hard to convince her fellow abolitionists to fight for the Fourteenth and Fifteenth Amendments to give women, in addition to African American men, the right to vote. However, male abolitionists did not agree, and said they should focus on African American suffrage for the time being.

Anthony and Stanton formed the National Woman Suffrage Association in 1869, and Anthony served as the organization's vice president for a time, before she was named president in 1892. Also founded in 1869 was the American Equal Rights Organization, in collaboration with Stanton and Douglass. When the organization voted as a whole to support the Fifteenth Amendment granting suffrage only to black men, Anthony decided to concentrate her energy solely on women's rights.

In 1872, Anthony and fifteen other Rochester women, including Anthony's mother and sisters, cast votes in the presidential election after persuading a poll worker that the Fourteenth Amendment had given equal rights to all citizens, and were arrested. Free on $1,000 bail (about $20,700 in 2018), Anthony was tried and convicted in 1873, and was fined $100 (about $2,000 in 2018). However, she refused to pay the fine. The judge did not make an effort to collect the fine so that she would not be allowed to appeal. Anthony protested in her defense:

It was we, the people, not we, the white male citizens, nor yet we, the male citizens; but we, the whole people, who formed this Union. And we formed it, not to give the blessings or liberty, but to secure them; not to the half of ourselves and the half of our posterity, but to the whole people—women as well as men. And it is downright mockery to talk to women of their enjoyment of the blessings of liberty while they are denied the use of the only means of securing them provided by this democratic-republican government—the ballot.

The only question left to be settled, now, is: Are women persons? And I hardly believe any of our opponents will have the hardihood to say they are not. Being persons, then, women are citizens, and no state has a right to make any new law, or to enforce any old law, that shall abridge their privileges or immunities. Hence, every discrimination against women in the constitutions and laws of the several states, is to-day null and void, precisely as is every one against negroes.[1]

Anthony's arrest would prove helpful in increasing awareness of the fact that women wanted the right to vote, enabling her and other suffragists to reach a larger audience.

Agreeing to Disagree

Anthony and Wells-Barnett became friends over the course of their political activism, and they also had a mutual friend in Frederick Douglass. Wells-Barnett stayed with Anthony when she traveled to Rochester in 1894. In her autobiography,

Wells-Barnett recalled an occurrence of Anthony springing to her defense:

> At the close of my address a young man in the audience, whom we afterward learned was a southerner, sneeringly asked, "If the colored people were so badly treated in the South, why was it that more of them didn't come North?" Before I could answer, Miss Anthony sprang to her feet and said, "I'll answer that question. It is because we, here in the North, do not treat the Negroes any better than they do in the South, comparatively speaking."[2]

Anthony then recounted for the audience an occurrence she had witnessed in the North about a young black girl who, although she attended an integrated school, was told she could not attend a school dance because she was not white. The dance had been advertised as open to all students, but when the girl attempted to get a ticket to attend, she was told that "all students" did not mean her.

In another instance involving Wells-Barnett, Anthony took a stand against racist behavior. During Wells-Barnett's stay, Anthony had instructed her secretary to assist the other woman with her correspondence. The stenographer refused to take dictation from a black woman, and Anthony promptly fired her.

The two women did not always see eye to eye. Anthony was single-minded in her fight for women's suffrage, believing that once women got the right to vote, they could resolve all other injustices. Wells-Barnett felt it would take much more than that to end racial inequality, and disagreed with Anthony's willingness to leave African American women out of NAWSA, which Anthony condoned out of concern for keeping white Southern women from leaving the organization and dooming the cause. Wells-Barnett lamented in her autobiography: "I felt that although she may have made gains for suffrage, she had also confirmed white women in their attitude of segregation."[3]

Despite this disagreement, Wells-Barnett considered Anthony a good friend, and Anthony gifted her with a signed copy of her biography, *The Life and Work of Susan B. Anthony*.

"Failure Is Impossible"

Anthony remained active until nearly the end of her life. At her final suffrage convention and eighty-sixth birthday celebration in Washington, DC, in 1906, she urged her guests to keep up the fight for women's suffrage, insisting, "Failure is impossible."[4] When Anthony died in Rochester on March 13, 1906, four states had given women the right to vote.

Jane Addams

Jane Addams was born on September 6, 1860, at the beginning of the Civil War, into a Quaker family in Cedarville, Illinois. She was the eighth of nine children. Her mother died in childbirth when Jane was only two. Her father was an abolitionist who served as an officer in the Civil War, was friends with Abraham Lincoln, and spent sixteen years as an Illinois state senator.

In 1877, Addams enrolled at Rockford Seminary, one of the first colleges for women. She graduated in 1881 but was not awarded her degree until 1882, after the school had been accredited as Rockford College for Women. She was among the first generation of women to graduate from college in the United States. While women in the late nineteenth century

Jane Addams, social reformer, feminist, and founder of Hull House, was partially responsible for a large number of reforms in the city of Chicago and the country as a whole.

were expected to take on family obligations after completing their education, Addams decided instead to attend medical school. However, this career choice was short lived. Soon after beginning school, Addams received word of her father's death and had to return home. In addition, she was experiencing tremendous pain from a crooked spine, and wound up bedridden for two years. Her spinal defect was repaired with surgery, but she was advised by her doctors to give up on returning to her studies.

After recovering from her surgery, Addams decided to begin traveling, and left for Europe. In 1888, during a trip to London with Ellen Gates Starr, a friend from Rockford, she visited Toynbee Hall, a settlement house in the slums of the East End. Toynbee Hall was one of the world's first settlement houses, founded by students at Oxford University, who used the institution to provide London's needy with education, a meeting room, a library, and other services.

Addams was inspired by Toynbee Hall. Her father had ingrained in her a sense of social responsibility, which had made her sympathetic to the less fortunate. She wanted to use her family's wealth to help the disadvantaged. Addams and Starr decided to open a settlement house in Chicago upon their return to the United States.

At this time, Chicago was full of impoverished European immigrants living in crowded tenements, often with no plumbing, and disease was rampant. Addams and Starr decided to rent a house in one of Chicago's industrial neighborhoods, which was a poor neighborhood and home to many of these immigrants. In 1889, they found an old brick mansion built by Charles Hull, which they rented as their settlement house. Addams admitted of the project: "We had no definite idea what we were there to do. But we hoped, by living among the people, to learn what was needed and to help out."[5]

Addams and Starr began raising money for their cause, persuaded other young women to volunteer, and cared for children and sick people in the neighborhood. Hull House became a success within a few years. It had a nursery and kindergarten for the children of working mothers, an evening coffee house, and social clubs. Over time, the institution drew more volunteers who taught English, music, and acting. Hull House had an art gallery, a labor museum, book bindery, a public kitchen, fitness facilities (including a swimming pool), a library, and an employment office. Many of the wealthy citizens of Chicago were impressed with the charitable work being done by Addams and others at Hull House, and began providing the settlement house with financial assistance.

By the 1900s, there were settlement houses in other major cities across the United States, and Addams had become famous worldwide for her creation of the settlement movement in America as well as her other social reform work. In addition to her work at Hull House, she was a lecturer and wrote many books and essays on democratic responsibility. In her 1902 work *Democracy and Social Ethics*, she wrote that one goal of democracy should be to "give voice to the opinions of common working people."[6] A feminist, Addams believed women had a duty and a right to be involved in politics for the good of democracy.

Wells-Barnett knew Addams from reform work in Chicago, and asked for her help in preventing the segregation of schools in the city. At Wells-Barnett's request, Addams gathered a meeting at Hull House to discuss the issue. Wells-Barnett wrote about the meeting in her autobiography:

I had asked Miss Addams to call them together and ask if the influential white citizens of Chicago would do for us what we could not do for ourselves …

As a result of this conference a committee of seven persons was appointed to wait upon the *Tribune*, and Miss Jane Addams was made chairman of that committee. I do not know what they did or what argument was brought to bear, but I do know that the series of articles ceased and from that day until this there has been no further effort made by the *Chicago Tribune* to separate the schoolchildren on the basis of race.[7]

Addams also worked for child labor laws and fought to eliminate overcrowded and unsanitary conditions in sweatshops. She was partially responsible for the establishment of juvenile courts and the 1893 Workshop and Factories Bill, which limited work hours in factories and restricted the use of child labor. In 1894, she even took a job as a garbage inspector, improving the garbage collection process so much that she was able to decrease the death rate of the neighborhood in which she worked.

In 1909, Addams attended the conference which would lead to the establishment of the NAACP, and she served as the vice president of NAWSA from 1911 to 1914. During World War I, Addams helped to organize the Women's International League for Peace and Freedom, which worked to end the war. She was an ardent advocate for peace and wrote about the impact of the war on immigrants. Her antiwar stance made her enemies, resulting in her being attacked in the press. However, she became popular again after the war because of her continued volunteer work.

Addams suffered a heart attack in 1926. On December 10, 1931, she was awarded the Nobel Peace Prize, but did not attend the ceremony to deliver the Nobel lecture, as she had been hospitalized and her doctor had advised her not to travel overseas. On May 21, 1935, at the age of seventy-five, Jane Addams died of cancer.

Mary Church Terrell

Mary "Mollie" Church, like Wells-Barnett, was born during the Civil War, on September 23, 1863. Her father, Robert Reed Church, was a former slave from Holly Springs and a friend of James Wells. He had moved to Memphis and became a wealthy property owner. Her mother, Louisa Ayers, owned a hair salon in Memphis before the couple divorced.

Church Terrell first encountered racism when she was very young. She was on a train with her father, who had gone to the smokers' car to socialize and left her in the first-class car alone for a brief time. The conductor tried to make Mollie move to the Jim Crow car. Fortunately for the young girl, her father soon returned. He could pass for a white man, and returned to the car with his pistol drawn to make the conductor leave young Mollie where she was.

Church Terrell began school in Memphis, but her mother was dissatisfied with the conditions of the school and sent her to Ohio for the remainder of her education. She attended Oberlin College and, after her parents' divorce, she split her vacations between New York and Memphis. Mollie and her brother were with their father in Memphis in 1879 when the yellow fever epidemic which killed Wells-Barnett's parents broke out. Robert Church sent his children back to New York, but he remained in Memphis. As people fled the city, he bought

Mary "Mollie" Church Terrell had a great deal in common with Ida B. Wells-Barnett, from their roots in Holly Springs and Memphis to their teaching careers, social activism, and involvement in women's clubs.

up abandoned real estate. When Memphis recovered, Church became the South's first black millionaire.

Church Terrell graduated from Oberlin in 1884, one of three African American women to receive a bachelor's of arts degree from the college that year. She returned to her father's house in Memphis, intending to become a teacher in the city. Her father forbade it, as he wanted her to act like a real Southern lady and look after his household until she got married and had a household of her own. However, after her father remarried the following year, she moved in with her mother in New York and applied for teaching positions. By the fall of 1885, Church Terrell had gotten a job teaching at Wilberforce University in Ohio. Later, she taught Latin in Washington's Colored High School, where she met Robert H. Terrell, a Harvard graduate.

Wells-Barnett met Church Terrell in Memphis at a social event in July 1887. Church Terrell's father had funded Wells-Barnett's trip back to Memphis from California. Although class differences likely kept them from becoming close friends, Wells-Barnett admired her greatly, and wrote in her diary after their introduction: "She is the first woman of my age I've met who is similarly inspired with the same desires hopes and ambitions."[8]

The two women had similar interests and goals, and were both active in the women's club movement. Unlike Wells-Barnett, Church Terrell had led a privileged life due to her parents' wealth, receiving a private education and a college degree. However, they both defied the expectations for women of the time by having careers and engaging in political activism. In addition, although she was advantaged, Church Terrell still faced racial prejudice, and, like Wells-Barnett, her experiences impacted her life and career as an activist. She too was a writer, although she had difficulty keeping it up due to her busy schedule, and some of her short stories and articles were rejected as controversial and never published.

Church Terrell's father sent her to Europe to study in 1888. She spent two years overseas, learning French, German, and Italian. In 1891, she returned to the United States to marry Robert Terrell. This was the end of her teaching career, as married women were not allowed to teach in most schools.

Like Ferdinand Barnett, Robert Terrell was very supportive of his wife's activism work. He was admitted to the bar shortly after their marriage, and later served as a judge of the Municipal Court of the District of Columbia for six four-year terms, until his death.

Like Wells-Barnett, Mary Church Terrell was also a friend of Thomas Moss. She was pregnant at the time of his lynching, and lost the baby soon after. As a result, she linked both tragedies in her mind. After Moss's murder, Church Terrell and Frederick Douglass visited the White House to ask President Benjamin Harrison to act against lynching. Douglass was a mentor to her as well as to Wells-Barnett.

Church Terrell was a leader in the National League of Colored Women, which was formed in 1895. The following year, the organization merged with the National Federation of African American Women to become the National Association of Colored Women. Wells-Barnett and Church Terrell met once more at the new organization's inaugural meeting in July, when Wells-Barnett was named the chairwoman of the Resolutions Committee and Terrell was elected the association's first president. Church Terrell also attended the founding conference of the NAACP and was named to the original "Founding Forty" list of individuals formally credited with the founding of the organization, while Wells-Barnett was not.

After the passage of the Nineteenth Amendment, Church Terrell began working to convince women to use their newly won right. She worked on the 1929 senatorial campaign for Ruth Hanna McCormick, the first woman to run for the United States Senate. In 1940, she published *A Colored Woman in a White World*, a book she had been working on for over twenty years. Mary Church Terrell died on July 24, 1954.

W. E. B. Du Bois

William Edward Burghardt ("W. E. B.") Du Bois was born in 1868, three years after the end of the Civil War, in Great Barrington, Massachusetts. His mother, Mary Burghardt Du Bois, was a domestic worker. His father, Alfred Du Bois, was a barber. He left the family when Du Bois was a young child. Great Barrington had been home to a very small African American community since before the American Revolution. Du Bois had very little exposure to the African American culture, as the local schools and church were primarily white.

In 1884, when Du Bois was sixteen, his mother died, which forced him to find employment in a local mill. He did not allow this to derail his education, and later that year he became the first African American to graduate from his Massachusetts high school. He spent the next three years attending Fisk University in Nashville, Tennessee, receiving his bachelor of arts degree in 1888.

During his time in Nashville, he experienced African American culture and also encountered racism that he had not experienced in Massachusetts. This would greatly impact his later social activism.

After graduating from Fisk, Du Bois moved back to New England to attend Harvard University and earned a second

Activist and sociologist W. E. B. Du Bois was one of the founding members of the Niagara Movement and the NAACP.

bachelor's degree in 1890 followed by a PhD in history in 1895, making him the first African American to receive a doctorate degree from Harvard. He also spent two years at the University of Berlin in Germany studying history and sociology, and published a dissertation entitled "The Suppression of the African Slave-Trade to the United States." He believed that college-educated African Americans had a duty to represent the interests of everyday people, and that this "talented tenth," as he called them, would improve African American economic conditions.[9] However, he also believed that without political rights, even with economic help, African Americans would always be vulnerable.

In 1896, Du Bois took a job at the University of Pennsylvania and gathered data for a sociological study of the African American community in the city. His study, *The Philadelphia Negro*, was published in 1899. This was the first comprehensive study of a black community in the United States. He moved back to the South in 1897 to become a professor of sociology at Atlanta University. For the next several years, Du Bois conducted research studies of various aspects of African American life in the rural South. He also wrote articles, novels, and nonfiction about the progress of African Americans, including *The Souls of Black Folk* in 1903.

At the beginning of the twentieth century, Du Bois decided to form an organization that would help African Americans coordinate protests for equal rights. In July 1905, he organized the first meeting of what would become the Niagara Movement, held in Niagara Falls, Canada. Twenty-nine people attended the three-day meeting, which met in Canada because no hotel on the American side of the falls would allow black customers, proving his point about the necessity of an organization of this kind. By the third day of the conference,

COMPROMISE AND ACCOMMODATION

Booker T. Washington was known for his accommodationist policy on racial issues, working within the Jim Crow system instead of openly fighting it. He encouraged a more passive approach to gaining political and civil rights rather than by struggle and protest, and believed that African Americans should focus on self-improvement, accepting segregation and establishing their own schools and businesses. The idea was that once they had advanced enough economically, whites would have to respect them and accept them as equals, giving them the political rights they wanted.

In 1895, Washington gave a speech at the Atlanta Cotton States and International Exposition, calling for African Americans to focus on self-help and exercise patience in waiting to achieve equality, stating:

> In all things that are purely social we can be as separate as the fingers, yet one as the hand in all things essential to mutual progress ... The wisest among my race understand that the agitation of questions of social equality is the extremist folly, and that progress in the enjoyment of all the privileges that will come to us must be the result of severe and constant struggle rather than of artificial forcing. No race that has anything to contribute to the markets of the world is long in any degree ostracized. It is important and right that all privileges of the law be ours, but it is vastly more important that we be prepared for the exercise of these privileges. The opportunity to earn a dollar in a factory just now is worth infinitely more than the opportunity to spend a dollar in an opera-house.[10]

This speech, commonly referred to as the "Atlanta Compromise," did not agree with the more confrontational style of his contemporaries Wells-Barnett and Du Bois, who vehemently opposed Washington's approach. While Wells-Barnett agreed that African Americans should try to better themselves economically, the lynching of Thomas Moss had shown her that economic advancement on its own would not make whites accept them. She believed that

Booker T. Washington (pictured) and Ida B. Wells-Barnett worked for the equality of African Americans everywhere, but they had differing opinions on how to achieve it.

action such as boycotts was necessary as well to force a change. She wrote disparagingly of Washington's approach:

> Our policy was to denounce the wrongs and injustices which were heaped upon our people, and to use whatever influence we had to help right them ... Mr. Washington's theory had been that we ought not to spend our time agitating for our rights; that we had better give attention to trying to be first-class people in a jim crow car than insisting that the jim crow car should be abolished ... And of course, fighting for political rights had no place whatsoever in his plans.[11]

Although he was accused by some of his colleagues of ignoring oppression, Washington secretly fought lynching and funded court cases against segregation and disenfranchisement.

the Niagara Movement had been founded as a protest organization. The attendees wrote a series of resolutions that blamed white supremacists alone for the continued low status of African Americans. They called for an end to segregation, racial violence, and disenfranchisement and demanded equal access to education, equality in economic opportunities, and equal treatment in the courts, particularly enforcement of the Fifteenth Amendment. The Niagara Movement continued to hold annual meetings until 1910.

On February 12, 1909, the one hundredth anniversary of Abraham Lincoln's birthday, Du Bois attended the National Negro Conference in New York City, along with most of the leaders from the Niagara Movement, including Wells-Barnett. At this conference, the NAACP was formed to fight for equal rights through legal action and nonviolent protest. Soon after, Du Bois resigned from his professor position to move to New York City and work out of the NAACP headquarters as the head of research and publicity. He also edited the organization's monthly publication, the *Crisis*.

Du Bois and Wells-Barnett shared a belief in the need for immediate action against racial injustice. They opposed Booker T. Washington's approach to the matter, opting for more visible and vigorous methods. While the two were acquainted with each other and exchanged correspondence, they were not very good friends. However, their mutual advocacy and beliefs inspired others to continue their cause even after they could no longer do so themselves.

In 1934, Du Bois resigned from the NAACP and returned to Atlanta University to teach. However, ten years later the university forced him into retirement because of a conflict with the school administrators. He was rehired by the NAACP but fired in 1948 for political reasons. He was banned from foreign travel by the government for several years due to his socialist leanings, but after the ban was lifted, Du Bois visited the Soviet Union, China, and Ghana. In 1961, he joined the Communist Party and then moved to Ghana to work on a research project. He renounced his American citizenship, becoming a citizen of Ghana in February 1963. Du Bois died later that year in Accra, Ghana.

CHAPTER FOUR

A Writer and an Activist

Wells-Barnett published many articles and editorials during the course of her career, most of them denouncing the practice of lynching. Three of her most important publications on lynching were *Southern Horrors*, *A Red Record*, and *Mob Rule in New Orleans*. In addition, she was involved in multiple social justice and reform organizations, the foremost being the NAACP, the Alpha Suffrage Club, and the Negro Fellowship League.

Publications on Lynching

In 1892, Wells-Barnett published *Southern Horrors: Lynch Law in All Its Phases*. This pamphlet compiled several of

This photo shows Ida B. Wells-Barnett with her four children, 1909.

her editorials from her lynching investigations that had been previously published in the *New York Age*. In *Southern Horrors*, she wrote about the lynching of her friend Thomas Moss and his colleagues, described as "peaceful, law-abiding citizens and energetic business men," on March 9, 1892, in Memphis.[1] The three men owned a grocery store on the opposite corner from another grocery store owned by a white man, Barrett, who led a group to attack the store. The owners shot at the attackers in self-defense, not realizing that some of them were police officers. The three men were jailed and then lynched. Authorities made no attempt to find and arrest the lynchers. Wells-Barnett detailed the horrific events and wrote of the lynching problem: "The strong arm of the law must be brought to bear upon lynchers in severe punishment, but this cannot and will not be done unless a healthy public sentiment demands and sustains such action."[2]

A Red Record: Tabulated Statistics and Alleged Causes of Lynching in the United States, 1892–1894, was published in 1895. In this pamphlet, Wells-Barnett included detailed records and statistics of lynchings over a two-year period, including names of the victims, dates of the events, places the lynchings occurred, and the motives for the killings. She used 1894 statistics from white-owned newspapers in her investigations of the causes of lynching, exposing lies about the supposed crimes of most lynch victims. She found that more often than not, innocent men were lynched. To justify the murders, the perpetrators and their supporters often claimed that lynch victims had raped white women, but Wells-Barnett found that this was almost always untrue. African Americans were lynched for "failing to pay debts, for perceived disrespect of white people, competing with white people economically and at times for consensual relationships with white people."[3] In some cases, a real relationship had been discovered between a white woman and an African American man, and the rape charges had been made in an effort to protect the woman's reputation.

Wells-Barnett included in *A Red Record* her explanation for its publication. Frequently, when she was advocating in public against lynching, she was asked for "facts and figures" to back up her accusations.[4] Her painstaking research was meant to do just that, both for her critics and her supporters. She wrote: "The very frequent inquiry made after my lectures by interested friends is 'What can I do to help the cause?' The answer always is: 'Tell the world the facts.' …The object of this publication is to tell the facts, and friends of the cause can lend a helping hand by aiding in the distribution of these books."[5]

In 1900, *Mob Rule in New Orleans* was published. In this publication, Wells-Barnett detailed the history of racial violence and lynching in the city of New Orleans. Specifically, she wrote about the murder of Robert Charles, who had fought back against police harassment that year and had been killed, inciting race riots in New Orleans: "Only by earnest, active, united endeavor to arouse public sentiment can we hope to put a stop to these demonstrations of American barbarism."[6]

Founding of the NAACP

On February 12, 1909, the one hundredth anniversary of Abraham Lincoln's birthday, Wells-Barnett attended the founding conference of the NAACP in New York, hoping that the group would work to eradicate lynching. She was one of the founding members but was viewed as a radical because of her opposition to Booker T. Washington's strategies.

While both Mary Church Terrell and W. E. B. Du Bois were named to the Committee of Forty, which had been appointed

Many African Americans who moved to Chicago from the South were impoverished, yet most social services agencies refused to help them. The recession of the 1920s led to increased unemployment rates. These buildings were housing for some people in Chicago during that time.

to oversee the formation of the organization, Wells-Barnett was left off of the Founding Forty list. This was despite having been told that she would be included. Many other founders objected to her exclusion and even offered to resign in order to make room for her on the committee. Eventually, because of those offers, she was added to the list. However, this made her feel patronized. She served on the NAACP's executive committee until 1912, then resigned because of a personality conflict with the chairman and other leadership within the organization.

The NAACP worked for improvements in housing, employment, and education, in addition to attempting to protect the rights of African Americans through the filing of lawsuits. The organization also adopted Wells-Barnett's antilynching cause. In 1918, the NAACP had gained recognition for its work against segregation and lynching, while Wells-Barnett was losing influence. Her distrust in and disappointment with the organization likely stemmed from the fact that later in her life, she was receiving hardly any public credit for her civil rights work.

Founding of the Alpha Suffrage Club

Wells-Barnett had joined the Women's Suffrage Association soon after her arrival in Illinois, but she had not succeeded in persuading the members of her women's club to join the movement until there was talk of limited suffrage for women in the state.

On January 30, 1913, Wells-Barnett founded the Alpha Suffrage Club, one of the women's suffrage organizations for African American women. It worked to mobilize black women throughout Chicago to fight for the vote. Her actions and those of other suffragists proved beneficial. Illinois passed the

Municipal and Presidential Voting Act later that year, which allowed women to vote in local and presidential elections.

Following the news, Wells-Barnett and the Alpha Suffrage Club began organizing black women to register to vote by showing them that, as Wells-Barnett wrote in her autobiography, "we could use our vote for the advantage of ourselves and our race."[7] Members of the Alpha Suffrage Club learned how to conduct door-to-door canvassing and campaigned throughout the Second Ward, one of Chicago's black neighborhoods, urging women to register to vote. By the registration deadline, 7,290 women in the Second Ward had registered. They succeeded in helping the Second Ward elect Chicago's first black alderman to the city council. They also raised money to send Wells-Barnett to represent them at the 1913 women's suffrage parade in Washington, DC. By 1916, the Alpha Suffrage Club had two hundred members.

Founding of the Negro Fellowship League

Wells-Barnett taught a Sunday school class for men aged eighteen to thirty during the early 1900s. Following the Springfield riot in 1908, during which several African Americans were killed and many more injured or driven out of town by a lynch mob, she was discussing the tragic events with these young men. Wells-Barnett wrote in her autobiography: "I told these young men that we should be bestirring ourselves to see what could be done. When one of them asked, 'What can we do about it?' I replied that they could at least get together and ask themselves that question."[8]

She then invited the class to come to her home and discuss what could be done. Three of them accepted her offer and began meeting regularly at her home, along with some of their

BRITISH SUPPORT

In the fall of 1892, one attendee of Wells-Barnett's antilynching lectures was British reformer Catherine Impey, who was visiting Frederick Douglass. Impey came from an abolitionist family and Wells-Barnett's antilynching work caught her attention. In 1893, Wells-Barnett was visiting Douglass, her friend and mentor, when she received an invitation from Impey to visit Great Britain and organize an antilynching campaign there. Encouraged by Douglass, Wells-Barnett left for Britain. She spent April and May of that year touring England, Scotland, and Wales, giving talks on lynching and Jim Crow laws.

Wells-Barnett's first trip was cut short due to a conflict between Impey and her other host, Isabelle Mayo. However, she returned to England in early 1894 to spend several more months there lecturing. During this second trip, she addressed large audiences in Liverpool, Manchester, Newcastle, and London, illustrating her speeches with newspaper accounts, letters, statistics, and photographs. She drew connections between the antislavery movement and the antilynching movement, hoping to remind the English of their previous support of abolition and persuade them to get involved against lynching. Wells-Barnett tried to persuade them that "they were in the unique position of being able to influence Americans," hoping that they would support her cause.[9]

As Wells-Barnett had hoped, many of the British people were in support. Former abolitionists began creating antilynching organizations. One such organization, the British Anti-Lynching Committee, wrote letters to Southern state governors in protest of lynching and even sent several of their members to the United States to investigate the situation in person.

Wells-Barnett returned to America from her second British tour after three months and over one hundred public appearances and lectures. The trip had led to increased attention from the press, as she had hoped, and she was featured in a larger number of newspapers than she had been prior to leaving the United States. She gave the British response credit for the decrease in lynching after 1893.

In addition to being successful, Wells-Barnett enjoyed her travels in Great Britain because of her positive interactions with the people she met: "It was indeed the most enjoyable feature of my nearly two years' association with the

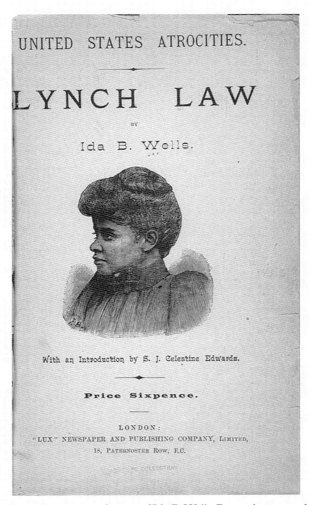

This is a London advertisement for one of Ida B. Wells-Barnett's overseas lectures on lynching in the American South. She considered her lecture series in England to be a great success.

British people—the absolute courtesy with which they treated those whom they considered worthy of being their guests. It was such an absolutely new thing to be permitted for once to associate with human beings who pay tribute to what they believe one possesses in the way of qualities of mind and heart, rather than to the color of the skin."[10]

friends, to discuss race matters. This was the beginning of the organization called the Negro Fellowship League, which Wells-Barnett and her Sunday school students formed to help African Americans in need and right the wrongs being done to them.

Before long, Wells-Barnett wanted to establish an organization that would help young men who came to Chicago and knew no one, who often ended up in trouble if they did not receive assistance. During this time, most social services agencies in Chicago, such as the YMCA and the Salvation Army, would not assist African Americans. In 1910, Wells-Barnett gave a speech about this injustice. One of the attendees of her lecture was the wife of Victor Lawson, who owned the *Chicago Daily News*. The Lawsons were major donors to the YMCA and were appalled to hear of the organization's exclusion of African Americans. They soon withdrew their funding and decided to support Wells-Barnett's establishment of the Negro Fellowship League Reading Room and Social Center, which opened on May 10 of that year.

The Negro Fellowship League ran a lodging house, employment agency, and reading room for African Americans in need of social services. Wells-Barnett had been inspired by Jane Addams's Hull House and hoped to obtain the same level of financial support for her organization, but unfortunately, that did not occur. The Negro Fellowship League was extremely underfunded for most of its ten years in existence. In 1913, the YMCA opened a facility for African Americans, and Lawson took his donations back to them. Unable to find a new donor, Wells-Barnett took a job as a parole officer in order to make enough money to keep the organization running.

The Negro Fellowship League was forced to close in 1920. Wells-Barnett had lost her parole officer job, and a recession in Chicago had resulted in high unemployment among African Americans. This made it difficult to keep the agency running. In addition, the work the organization did was being replaced by the black branch of the YMCA, state-funded employment agencies, and the Chicago Urban League. Despite its financial problems, the Negro Fellowship League was Wells-Barnett's "longest-lasting and most satisfying organizational commitment."[11]

A dedicated and resourceful woman, Wells-Barnett held firmly to her beliefs and principles despite setbacks. Although she was often not given due credit, her influence was nonetheless strong. Her work on lynching, social issues, and community development was carried on by a number of organizations and individuals, even after her death.

CHAPTER FIVE

⌒

Positive and Negative Reputation

Between 1890 and 1931, Wells-Barnett was described in a variety of newspapers, magazines, journals, and books as being determined, passionate, and often aggressive in her pursuit of social justice. Depending on the source, these traits could be viewed as either positive or negative. She made both friends and enemies through her activism, but never stopped fighting hard for her goals and beliefs.

Praise

By Wells-Barnett's thirtieth birthday, her reputation as a powerful writer had led to her becoming a trusted and inspiring journalist. Her exposure of lynching had

Judge Albion W. Tourgee inspired
the founding of the Tourgee Club.

contributed to that reputation. The women of New York City who organized her testimonial at Lyric Hall on October 5, 1892, had believed in her and supported her cause, even raising money to help advance her career.

Because of her in-depth investigations of lynching, newspapers other than the several she was involved in personally began hiring her to investigate more instances of lynching. In 1898, after the horrific lynching of a black postmaster in South Carolina, a group of prominent African Americans in Chicago funded a trip to Washington, DC, for Wells-Barnett in order for her to lobby for antilynching legislation. Although in the end nothing was done to attempt to find and prosecute the postmaster's murderers, Wells-Barnett managed to persuade President McKinley to meet with her to discuss the issue. In 1890, she was sent to conduct an in-depth investigation into another lynching in Missouri.

Another accomplishment for which Wells-Barnett received positive acclaim was her organization of the first African American women's club in Illinois. In 1893, African American men in Chicago had formed the Tourgee Club, which had scheduled a weekly "Ladies' Day" to include women in the organization. Attendance at this weekly event was sparse until Wells-Barnett got involved. After she managed to increase attendance by giving lectures at Ladies' Day, the attendees decided to form a women's club. They named the organization after the woman who had inspired them, founding the Ida B. Wells Club in September 1893. By the following February, the club had over three hundred members. Wells-Barnett maintained a strong belief in the power of women's clubs throughout her life, trusting that they could accomplish a great deal of reform.

Wells-Barnett also achieved some success in her work to end lynching, although she would see no federal legislation.

Her speeches abroad had brought increased attention to the cause, which resulted in debates in Congress and the passage of antilynching laws in a few states. Between 1893 and 1897, North Carolina, Georgia, South Carolina, Ohio, Kentucky, and Texas all enacted laws of varying severity intending to protect prisoners in custody and punish mob violence. While these antilynching laws were not strongly enforced, their passage did demonstrate an increased level of public outcry over lynching.

Wells-Barnett was honored in the spring of 1927 for her achievements, along with her husband. The Ida B. Wells Club hosted the couple as guests of honor at a dinner to celebrate Wells-Barnett, the "Mother of all clubs."[1] One guest maintained that the city of Chicago owed more to the Barnetts for the improvement of racial conditions in the city than to anyone else.

Criticism

Her outspoken nature and determination in the fight against lynching had negative consequences as well. She once had to turn down a job as a regular lecturer at the Slayton Lyceum Bureau since the offer was conditional upon her leaving out discussions of lynching, and her sense of personal integrity would not allow her to do it. In 1892, her editorial campaign against lynching led to the destruction of the *Free Speech* office, and the mob that had destroyed the newspaper's office threatened her life as well. Wells-Barnett was essentially exiled from the city of Memphis due to these events, and was forced to remain in the North, where she published editorials for the *New York Age* recounting her tale.

On December 15, 1892, the *Memphis Commercial* newspaper attacked Wells-Barnett in a vicious editorial,

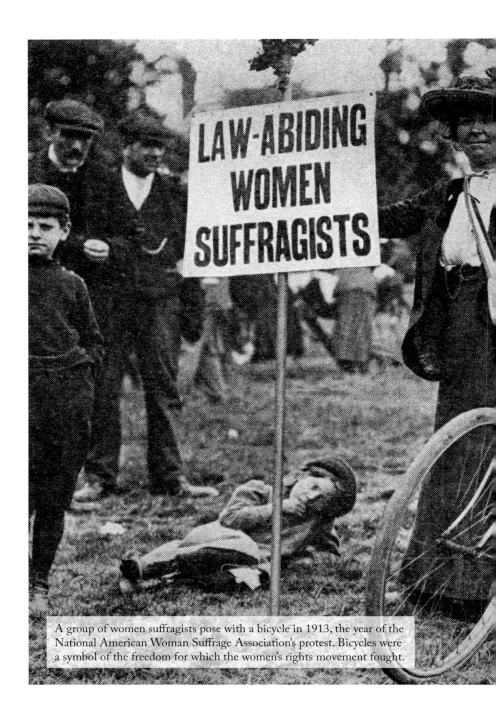

A group of women suffragists pose with a bicycle in 1913, the year of the National American Woman Suffrage Association's protest. Bicycles were a symbol of the freedom for which the women's rights movement fought.

calling her a fraud and a harlot and accusing her of fabricating her story of exile and raising money for her personal use. The article slandered her character, questioning both her morals and her professional integrity through implications that one of her business partners had actually written the editorial that led to her exile, and that she was secretly his mistress. She went to Albion Tourgee, a friend and a judge, asking him for legal advice as she wanted to sue the *Commercial* for libel. Tourgee referred her to Chicago lawyer Ferdinand Barnett, the man she would eventually marry. Barnett agreed to represent her, but after his initial investigation, in which he confirmed both her story and her character, the two decided against the lawsuit out of fear it would result in a negative impact on her work against lynching.

Wells-Barnett had a habit of picking unpopular battles, and her reputation for being outspoken and at times unpredictable frequently resulted in the alienation of her colleagues. She was often thought of as a troublemaker, and as a result, "she was never fully appreciated for her political acumen and repeatedly edged out of any leading role in the civil rights initiatives that she helped launch."[2] She was excluded from an 1899 meeting of the National Association of Colored Women when Mary Church Terrell was told that many Chicago women would not participate in the event if Wells-Barnett was invited. She was also initially left out of the founding committee of the NAACP, although she was added after an uproar from some of her supporters on the committee. The NAACP would go on to adopt Wells-Barnett's cause and some of her methods while simultaneously marginalizing her. This led to her distrust of many of her fellow African American civil rights leaders.

Segregation at the Suffrage Parade

During the second half of the 1800s, there was a great deal of overlap in members of the women's rights and abolitionist movements. However, a rift was created between these two groups of activists following the Civil War. Particularly, women's rights supporters had split over whether or not they should fight to include women in the Fifteenth Amendment on voting rights. Many female abolitionists who were also women's rights activists were upset when the Fourteenth and Fifteenth Amendments allowed black men to vote but not women.

This was the official program art for the National American Woman Suffrage Association (NAWSA) march for women's suffrage in Washington, DC, on March 3, 1913, which Wells-Barnett attended.

THE WORLD'S COLUMBIAN EXPOSITION

In the summer of 1893, the World's Columbian Exposition was held in Chicago to commemorate the four hundredth anniversary of Christopher Columbus arriving in America, celebrating American achievement since 1492. Exposition officials had rejected all exhibit proposals from or about African Americans, mostly limiting their representation to a single "Colored People's Day." Wells-Barnett, among other leaders in the black community, found this insulting and felt it would perpetuate stereotypes and further emphasize segregation.

Several of these leaders came together at the exposition to collaborate on a pamphlet, titled *The Reason Why the Colored American Is Not in the World's Columbian Exposition*, which was intended to educate the public on the unfairness of the situation, and to serve as a statement against lynching and segregation. The four coauthors were Frederick Douglass, Wells-Barnett, Ferdinand Barnett, and historian I. Garland Penn. The publication provided a "history of racial attitudes formed during slavery," including legal injustice and discriminatory post-Reconstruction laws.[3]

Frederick Douglass provided the introduction to the work. In it he discussed the efforts of the African American people to improve their lives once freed, and the truth of how blacks were still treated after emancipation. He upheld that the impact of slavery could still be felt, and was, in fact, the reason why African Americans had been excluded from representation in the exposition. He wrote: "Let the truth be told, let the light be turned on ignorance and prejudice, let lawless violence and murder be exposed."[4]

Wells-Barnett contributed two chapters about the history and statistics of lynching. In her first chapter, "Class Legislation," she discussed the disenfranchisement of African Americans in the South: "We were liberated not only empty-handed but left in the power of a people who resented our emancipation ... They were therefore armed with a motive for doing everything in their power to render our freedom a curse rather than a blessing."[5] She went on to write about how the Southern states used intimidation as a method of disenfranchising African Americans, knowing that depriving them of their right to vote would leave the country controlled by whites. In her second chapter, "Lynch

Many impressive structures were built for the World's Columbian Exposition in the summer of 1893. It celebrated American achievement since the arrival of Christopher Columbus in 1492.

Law," she cited academic research, reports from white-owned newspapers, and her own investigations in a discussion of the excuses given for lynching.

Ferdinand Barnett, Wells-Barnett's future husband, concluded with his chapter, "The Reason Why." He wrote about the desire among African Americans to show the world how much they had improved their condition since slavery had ended, viewing the exposition as "their first opportunity to show what freedom and citizenship can do for a slave."[6] He discussed the attempts made by African American leaders to gain participation in the planning of the event, and their disappointment in being given neither representation nor influence. Barnett put the blame for this directly upon the white planners of the exposition, emphasizing: "Our failure to be represented is not of our own working."[7]

Unfortunately, people mostly took little notice of the pamphlet. It did not affect exposition attendance, and many African Americans even worried that the authors' intent would backfire and increase racism. While twenty thousand copies of the pamphlet were printed, the publication did not have the impact its authors had hoped it would.

This rift may have led to an element of racism within the women's suffrage movement. At times, some suffragists expressed frustration over the fact that illiterate black men had the right to vote while educated white women did not. Some, particularly in the South, tried to gain more support for the cause by arguing that granting women the right to vote would help white voters outnumber non-whites. As a result, clubs that formed in support of women's suffrage frequently denied admittance to African American women. Wells-Barnett challenged segregation within the movement when the National American Woman Suffrage Association did not.

The National American Woman Suffrage Association held a protest in Washington, DC, on March 13, 1913, right before the inauguration of Woodrow Wilson. The protest took the form of a march down Pennsylvania Avenue, with five thousand suffragists dressed in white carrying banners and floats showing the history of the movement. Wells-Barnett attended as part of the delegation of sixty-two members from Illinois. She was told by NAWSA leaders that black suffragists were to march together in the back of the parade, instead of with their state contingents. This was a gesture meant to appease Southern white members of the club who did not want to march with black women.

Wells-Barnett naturally objected to this segregation of the suffrage protest, but outwardly gave in to the request. However, she disappeared from the black contingent shortly before the parade began. When the Illinois delegation began to march, Wells-Barnett emerged from the crowd along with two of her supporters and joined her compatriots, defying the segregation order from NAWSA leadership. Her nerve won her great praise from many of the newspapers that covered the event.

Wells-Barnett was known for being uncompromising. This sometimes caused problems for her personally, but ultimately it would impact her causes in a positive way. Her refusal to accept racism within the women's suffrage movement encouraged more women of color to join the movement and fight for equal rights. In addition, by reporting on instances of lynching in detail and exposing its true causes, she raised awareness and was able to sway public opinion against the horrific practice. The volume of information she gathered through her research and investigation eventually led to a decline in lynching, although no federal legislation would be enacted.

CHAPTER SIX

The Legacy of a Social Justice Warrior

W ells-Barnett believed strongly that "ideals had to be fought for," and never lost faith in hers.[1] While she did not succeed in eradicating lynching during her lifetime, the practice had been exposed and did decrease slightly because of her actions. She had succeeded in amassing "an invaluable store of information that would eventually help turn the tide against lynching."[2]

Temporarily Overlooked But Not Forgotten

Although she achieved several firsts for African American women, Wells-Barnett was mostly underappreciated during her lifetime. She was never fully accepted into

This photograph of Ida B. Wells-Barnett was taken during the final years of her career.

most of the organizations she helped start and frequently not given due credit for her achievements in civil rights and women's suffrage. She was aware of this, and decided to write her autobiography partially because she feared her public career had been forgotten before it had even ended: "All at once the realization came to me that I had nothing to show for all those years of toil and labor."[3] However, her primary reason for writing was the following, in her own words:

> The history of this entire period which reflected glory on the race should be known. Yet most of it is buried in oblivion and only the southern white man's misrepresentations are in the public libraries and college textbooks of the land. The black men who made the history of that day were too modest to write of it, or did not realize the importance of the written word to their posterity.
>
> And so, because our youth are entitled to the facts of race history which only the participants can give, I am thus led to set forth the facts contained in this volume which I dedicate to them.[4]

For several decades following her death, Wells-Barnett and her achievements remained mostly neglected by historians. She was not entirely forgotten, as her memory was kept alive through Ida B. Wells clubs across the country, and in 1950 Chicago named her to a list of twenty-five outstanding women in the city's history. However, for the most part, her accomplishments in both civil rights and women's suffrage were overlooked until later in the twentieth century.

In 1970, her daughter Alfreda Duster completed and published her mother's unfinished autobiography, titled

Alfreda Barnett Duster was the youngest daughter of Ida B. Wells-Barnett and Ferdinand Barnett. Duster completed and published her mother's unfinished autobiography, *Crusade for Justice*, in 1970.

URBAN REFORM WORK IN CHICAGO AND THE IDA B. WELLS HOMES

After 1910, Wells-Barnett became very active in an effort to solve social problems in Chicago, including segregation of schools and neighborhoods, public discrimination and attacks on civil liberties, and the "relentless policing" of African Americans who had recently relocated from the South to seek work.[5] She founded the Negro Fellowship League to assist African American men and the Alpha Suffrage Club to organize African American women to vote. In addition, Wells-Barnett established the first kindergarten for African American children in the city of Chicago, with the help of the Ida B. Wells Club, and collaborated with Jane Addams to block the establishment of segregated schools.

After her death, she was commemorated for her work with the poor by the Chicago Housing Authority, which named a low-cost apartment complex after her. The Ida B. Wells Homes were built around 1940. The housing complex was demolished in 2002 due to disrepair, but in its day it was an ideal location for families. The site may one day be home to a monument built in her honor.

This photograph, taken in 1942, shows the Ida B. Wells Homes, a Chicago low-income housing project. The housing project was named after Wells-Barnett because of her work with Chicago's poor.

Crusade for Justice. Wells-Barnett had kept various articles, letters, written speeches, printed pamphlets, photographs, and newspaper clippings, all of which helped Duster complete the story of her life.

Interest in her life and accomplishments had increased as the civil rights era of the 1950s and 1960s had begun, and peaked with the beginning of the black feminist movement of the 1970s and the discovery of previously neglected African American women's history. Duster published her mother's autobiography at an ideal time, when both black history and women's history were finally beginning to receive the attention they deserved.

Wells-Barnett's work helped to "shape twentieth-century civil rights activism," and she is recognized today for her journalism skills, her engagement of African American women in the suffrage movement, and for raising awareness of lynching.[6]

Commemoration at Last

The Chicago house where the Barnetts resided from 1919 to 1930 became a national landmark in 1974. In 1989, Wells-Barnett was featured in a PBS documentary called *Ida B. Wells: A Passion for Justice*, directed by William Greaves, as part of the American Experience series. The United States Postal Service featured her picture on a postage stamp in 1990.

In 1988, five of Wells-Barnett's grandchildren founded the Ida B. Wells Memorial Foundation to preserve her legacy. The foundation provides support to the Ida B. Wells-Barnett Museum located in her birthplace of Holly Springs, along with a multitude of other organizations and programs related to education, journalism, and racial equality. Through the

This is a photograph of the Barnetts' home in Chicago, taken in 2007. The family lived here from 1919 to 1930, moving shortly before Wells-Barnett's death. The house was named a national landmark in 1974.

foundation, Wells-Barnett's descendants travel to give speeches at museums and other organizations about her life and the issues near to her heart.

In 2011, a monument to Wells-Barnett was proposed for construction in Chicago. The Ida B. Wells Memorial Foundation intends to support the construction of this monument, under the guidance of the Ida B. Wells Commemorative Art Committee.

Ida B. Wells–Barnett: Suffragette and Social Activist

This is the Ida B. Wells-Barnett Museum in Holly Springs, Mississippi, Ida B. Wells-Barnett's birthplace. The museum is supported by a foundation formed by her grandchildren, who carry on her legacy.

This monument would be built in a park in Wells-Barnett's old neighborhood in Chicago, and would be donated to the City of Chicago's Public Art Collection once completed. The details of the monument's appearance have been left to the proposed sculptor, Richard Hunt. As of 2018, efforts to finish raising money for the production of the monument were still under way.

The Ida B. Wells Scholarship and Donald L. Duster Scholarship are both awarded to exceptional students each year. The Ida B. Wells Scholarship is awarded to three students at Rust College in Holly Springs, the same school Wells-Barnett attended. It is given to students who excel academically and demonstrate excellent leadership skills. The Donald L. Duster Scholarship is named after Wells-Barnett's grandson, who was a founder of the Ida B. Wells Memorial Foundation and followed in his grandmother's footsteps with his support of services to help underprivileged urban populations. This scholarship is awarded once per year at the University of Illinois at Urbana–Champaign, which Duster attended.

A recent addition to Well-Barnett's legacy is the Ida B. Wells Society for Investigative Reporting, founded in 2015 by Nikole Hannah-Jones, Ron Nixon, Corey Johnson, and Topher Sanders, four black journalists who were concerned about the lack of people of color in the field of investigative journalism, as well as the lack of support in newsrooms for investigative work. They started the Society for Investigative Reporting to train, mentor, and support journalists of color who want to do investigative reporting and help them acquire the tools they need to succeed in their positions. Inspired by Wells-Barnett's work, this organization seeks to carry on her social justice legacy by educating today's journalists. Their headquarters are in New York City at the City University of New York Graduate School of Journalism.

Toward the end of her life, Wells-Barnett struggled with concern over being forgotten, afraid she would have nothing to show for her life's work. Despite her fears, she had accomplished a great deal. She was the editor of multiple newspapers over her lifetime, at a time when few African American women held such leadership roles. Although lynching decreased only slightly during her life, she had provided the tools to continue its decline. The work of organizations such as the NAACP, inspired by her tactics, would yield results, as the NAACP was able to reach a wider audience due to its increased prominence. Wells-Barnett inspired later African American leaders in the civil rights movement of the 1960s, several decades after her death, and has been an inspiration to the investigative journalists of the twenty-first century.

CHRONOLOGY

1862 Ida Bell Wells is born in Holly Springs, Mississippi.

1868 The Fourteenth Amendment is ratified, giving American citizenship to former slaves.

1870 The Fifteenth Amendment is ratified, giving African American men the right to vote.

1875 The Civil Rights Act is passed, giving African Americans the right to sue over race discrimination in public places.

1878 The "Susan B. Anthony Amendment," which would give women the right to vote, is introduced in Congress for the first time and does not pass. Wells-Barnett's parents and youngest brother die in a yellow fever epidemic and she takes responsibility for raising her remaining siblings, beginning work as a teacher.

1881 Wells-Barnett moves to Memphis, Tennessee.

1883 The Civil Rights Act of 1875 is ruled unconstitutional. Wells-Barnett is forcibly removed from a train for refusing to leave the first-class car and files a lawsuit against the railroad.

1886 Wells-Barnett becomes editor of the *Evening Star*.

1889 Wells-Barnett is invited to write for the *Memphis Free Speech and Headlight*, buys a one-third interest in the paper and becomes editor.

1891 Wells-Barnett writes an editorial protesting the conditions of segregated schools in Memphis and loses her teaching job as a result.

1892 Thomas Moss and his business partners, Will Stewart and Calvin McDowell, are lynched. Wells-Barnett publishes an editorial on lynching. A mob destroys the *Free Speech* office and Wells-Barnett moves to New York. She publishes *Southern Horrors: Lynch Law in All Its Phases.*

1893 The World's Columbian Exposition is held in Chicago and Wells-Barnett and others publish *The Reason Why the Colored American Is Not in the World's Columbian Exposition.* Wells-Barnett moves to Chicago, joins the staff of the *Chicago Conservator*, and founds the Ida B. Wells Club.

1895 Wells-Barnett becomes the editor of the *Conservator.* She marries Ferdinand Barnett and becomes Ida B. Wells-Barnett. She publishes *A Red Record: Tabulated Statistics and Alleged Causes of Lynching in the United States, 1892–1894.*

1896 In *Plessy v. Ferguson*, the Supreme Court rules that "separate but equal" conditions are allowed under the Fourteenth Amendment.

1900 Wells-Barnett publishes *Mob Rule in New Orleans.*

1905 W. E. B. Du Bois organizes the first meeting of the Niagara Movement in Niagara Falls, Canada.

1909 Wells-Barnett attends the founding conference of the National Association for the Advancement of Colored People in New York.

1910 Wells-Barnett starts the Negro Fellowship League, a rooming house and social center.

1913 Illinois passes the Municipal and Presidential Voting Act allowing women to vote in municipal and presidential elections. Wells-Barnett founds the Alpha Suffrage Club. Five thousand suffragists march in Washington, DC, the day before Woodrow Wilson's inauguration.

1920 The Nineteenth Amendment is ratified, giving women the right to vote. The Negro Fellowship League closes. Wells-Barnett is diagnosed with gallstones and undergoes surgery.

1930 Wells-Barnett runs for election to the Illinois state senate and loses.

1931 Wells-Barnett dies of kidney disease.

GLOSSARY

abolitionist A person who supported the end of slavery in the United States.

accommodationist A person who adapts to the views of his or her opposition.

alderman An elected member of a municipal council.

assimilation The process by which a person takes on the social characteristics of a culture.

canvassing An attempt to gain political support or votes for political campaigns.

disenfranchisement The state of being deprived of the right to vote.

Exodusters The name given to African Americans who migrated to Kansas during the late nineteenth century.

extradition The giving up of an alleged criminal to another state or country at its request.

grandfather clause A provision designed to disenfranchise blacks while allowing whites to vote by permitting descendants of men voting before 1867 to vote without meeting certain other conditions.

habeas corpus A law stating that a person under arrest cannot be kept in prison without having been brought before a judge or court.

Jim Crow A name given to the series of laws discriminating against African Americans and requiring segregation.

lyceum An institution providing lectures, discussions, concerts, and similar educational programs.

lynching The illegal execution of an individual by a mob without a trial.

marginalizing Treating a person as powerless or insignificant.

muckrakers Journalists who seek out and expose scandal.

National American Woman Suffrage Association (NAWSA) An organization that fought for women's suffrage.

National Association for the Advancement of Colored People (NAACP) A civil rights organization founded to fight racial discrimination.

New Deal A group of government programs designed to improve economic and social conditions after the Great Depression.

Niagara Movement A civil rights group that fought for social and political rights for African Americans.

picketing Standing or marching near a location as part of a protest.

pro bono Work done without charge, especially legal work for clients with low income.

Progressive Era A period of social and political reform in the United States from the 1890s to the 1920s.

prohibition The forbidding by law of the sale and manufacture of alcohol in the United States under the Eighteenth Amendment.

ratify To sign or formally approve a law, such as a constitutional amendment.

Reconstruction The period following the Civil War when the states of the Confederacy were brought back into the United States.

Reconstruction Acts Laws of Congress passed from 1865 to 1877 outlining the conditions under which Southern states must rejoin the Union.

segregation The enforced separation of racial groups.

settlement house An institution providing social services to an urban community.

sharecropping A system of farming under which landowners rented sections of their land to farmers in return for a share of the crops produced on the land.

suffrage The right to vote in political elections.

sweatshop A factory or workshop requiring employees to work for long hours and low wages under poor conditions.

temperance Moderation in or abstinence from drinking alcohol.

testimonial A public tribute to a person and their achievements.

Versailles Peace Conference The meeting of the Allied powers after the end of World War I to set the terms of peace.

SOURCES

CHAPTER ONE

1. "The Constitution of the United States of America: Analysis and Interpretation," Constitution Annotated, Accessed March 6, 2018, https://www.congress.gov/constitution-annotated.

2. Ibid.

3. Lawrence Goldstone, *Inherently Unequal: The Betrayal of Equal Rights by the Supreme Court, 1865–1903* (New York: Walker & Company, 2011), 133.

4. Tamar Rothenburg, "The Long Battle for Women's Equality," *Scholastic Update*, May 18, 1987, http://link.galegroup.com/apps/doc/A4839270/AONE?u=nysl_we_becpl&sid=AONE&xid=c070076f.

CHAPTER TWO

1. Miriam DeCosta-Willis, ed., *The Memphis Diary of Ida B. Wells* (Boston, MA: Beacon Press, 1995), 140-141.

2. Alfreda M. Duster, ed., *Crusade for Justice: The Autobiography of Ida B. Wells* (Chicago, IL: The University of Chicago Press, 1970), 47–48.

3. Ibid., 64.

4. Ibid., 79.

5. Ibid., 249.

CHAPTER THREE

1. Susan B. Anthony, "Is It A Crime To Vote?" Accessed March 3, 2018, http://www.pbs.org/stantonanthony/resources/index.html?body=crime_to_vote.html.

2. Duster, *Crusade*, 227.

3. Ibid., 230.

4. "Susan Brownell Anthony," in *World of Sociology*, Accessed March 2, 2018, http://link.galegroup.com/apps/doc/K2427100065/BIC?u=buffalo_main&sid=BIC&xid=906554fc.

5. Mark Kornblatt and Pamela Renner, "'Saint' Jane," *Scholastic Update*, February 23, 1990, http://link.galegroup.com/apps/doc/A8560279/AONE?u=nysl_we_becpl&sid=AONE&xid=f4644eb5.

6. "Jane Addams," in *Feminist Writers*, edited by Pamela Kester-Shelton (Detroit, MI: St. James Press, 1996), Accessed March 4, 2018, http://link.galegroup.com/apps/doc/K2410000003/BIC?u=buffalo_main&sid=BIC&xid=dc4cae17.

7. Duster, *Crusade*, 277–278.

8. DeCosta-Willis, *The Memphis Diary of Ida B. Wells*, 150.

9. Pierre Hauser, *Great Ambitions: 1896–1909*, (New York: Chelsea House, 2015), http://online.infobase.com/HRC/Source/Details/5?sourceId=100426.

10. Booker T. Washington, "Speech to the Atlanta Cotton States and International Exposition Atlanta, Georgia - September 18, 1895," Accessed March 3, 2018, http://americanradioworks.publicradio.org/features/sayitplain/btwashington.html.

11. Duster, *Crusade*, 265.

CHAPTER FOUR

1. Ida B. Wells-Barnett, *On Lynching*, introduction by Patricia Hill Collins, (Amherst, NY: Humanity Books, 2002), 44.

2. Ibid., 49.

3. "The Ida B. Wells Society for Investigative Reporting," Accessed March 7, 2018, http://idabwellssociety.org.

4. Wells-Barnett, *On Lynching*, 151.

5. Ibid.

6. Wells-Barnett, *On Lynching*, 201.

7. Duster, *Crusade*, 345.

8. Ibid., 299.

9. Paula J. Giddings, *Ida: A Sword Among Lions*, (New York: Amistad, 2008), 286.

10. Duster, *Crusade*, 212.

11. Mia Bay, *To Tell the Truth Freely: The Life of Ida B. Wells*, (New York: Hill and Wang, 2009), 294.

CHAPTER FIVE

1. Giddings, *A Sword Among Lions*, 641.

2. Bay, *To Tell the Truth Freely*, 235.

3. Giddings, *A Sword Among Lions*, 278.

4. Ida B. Wells, Frederick Douglass, Irvine Garland Penn, and Ferdinand L. Barnett, *The Reason Why the Colored American Is Not in the World's Columbian Exposition*, edited by Robert W. Rydell (Urbana, IL: University of Illinois Press, 1999), 15.

5. Ibid., 17.

6. Ibid., 65.

7. Ibid., 81.

CHAPTER SIX

1. Giddings, *A Sword Among Lions*, 654–665.

2. Hauser, *Great Ambitions*.

3. Duster, *Crusade*, 414.

4. Ibid., 5.

5. Bay, *To Tell the Truth Freely*, 238.

6. Ibid., 285.

FURTHER INFORMATION

BOOKS

Bay, Mia, ed. *The Light of Truth: Writings of An Anti-Lynching Crusader*. New York: Penguin Publishing Group, 2014.

Burroughs, Todd Steven. *Warrior Princess: A People's Biography of Ida B. Wells*. New York: Diasporic Africa Press, 2017.

Davidson, James West. *"They Say": Ida B. Wells and the Reconstruction of Race*. New York: Oxford University Press, 2008.

Gottlieb, Julie V., ed. *Feminism and Feminists After Suffrage*. New York: Routledge, 2016.

Hill, DaMaris B., ed. *The Fluid Boundaries of Suffrage and Jim Crow: Staking Claims in the American Heartland*. Lanham, MD: Lexington Books, 2016.

WEBSITES

The Ida B. Wells Memorial Foundation
http://www.ibwfoundation.org

The Ida B. Wells Memorial Foundation, founded by five of Wells-Barnett's grandchildren, supports the Ida B. Wells-Barnett Museum. The foundation works to preserve Wells-Barnett's legacy by supporting organizations that promote education, journalistic integrity, and social justice.

The Ida B. Wells Society for Investigative Reporting
http://idabwellssociety.org

The Ida B. Wells Society for Investigative Reporting works to increase the number of people of color working in investigative reporting. They are committed to demonstrating the importance of diversity in the field of investigative journalism.

National Women's History Museum
https://www.nwhm.org

The NWHM is a nonprofit organization that seeks to open a museum at the National Mall in Washington, DC, alongside the other national museums. Their goal is to better integrate women's history into American history as a whole.

MUSEUMS

Ida B. Wells-Barnett Museum
220 North Randolph Street
Holly Springs, MS 38635

National Civil Rights Museum
450 Mulberry St.
Memphis, TN 38103

National Women's History Museum
Administrative Offices
205 S. Whiting Street Suite 254
Alexandria, VA 22304

Women's Rights National Historic Park
136 Fall Street
Seneca Falls, NY 13148

BIBLIOGRAPHY

Anderson, Amy. "One Woman's Voice: Susan B. Anthony Inspired a National Movement for Equality." *Success*, May 2009. *Biography In Context*. http://link.galegroup.com/apps/doc/A197935846/BIC?u=buffalo_main&sid=BIC&xid=5d2ad5e.

Anthony, Susan B. "Is It A Crime To Vote?" Accessed March 3, 2018. http://www.pbs.org/stantonanthony/resources/index.html?body=crime_to_vote.html.

Bay, Mia. *To Tell the Truth Freely: The Life of Ida B. Wells*. New York: Hill and Wang, 2009.

Blackmon, Douglas A. *Slavery By Another Name: The Re-Enslavement of Black Americans from the Civil War to World War II*. New York: Doubleday, 2008.

"The Constitution of the United States of America: Analysis and Interpretation." Constitution Annotated. Accessed March 6, 2018. https://www.congress.gov/constitution-annotated.

DeCosta-Willis, Miriam, ed. *The Memphis Diary of Ida B. Wells*. Boston, MA: Beacon Press, 1995.

Dray, Philip. *Capitol Men: The Epic Story of Reconstruction Through the Lives of the First Black Congressmen*. New York: Houghton Mifflin Company, 2008.

Duster, Alfreda M., ed. *Crusade for Justice: The Autobiography of Ida B. Wells*. Chicago, IL: The University of Chicago Press, 1970.

"14th Amendment to the Constitution Was Ratified." America's Story from America's Library. http://www. americaslibrary.gov/jb/recon/jb_recon_revised_1.html.

"Freedmen's Organizations and Agencies." in *DISCovering Multicultural America: African Americans, Hispanic Americans, Asian Americans, Native Americans*. Detroit, MI: Gale, 2003. Academic OneFile. http://link.galegroup. com/apps/doc/EJ2116200113/AONE?u=nysl_we_ becpl&sid=AONE&xid=5d8233fe.

Giddings, Paula J. *Ida: A Sword Among Lions*. New York: Amistad, 2008.

Goldstone, Lawrence. *Inherently Unequal: The Betrayal of Equal Rights by the Supreme Court, 1865–1903*. New York: Walker & Company, 2011.

Hauser, Pierre. *Great Ambitions: 1896–1909*. New York: Chelsea House, 2015.

Henry, Christopher E. *Forever Free: 1863–1875*. New York: Chelsea House, 2015.

"The Ida B. Wells Memorial Foundation." Accessed March 6, 2018. http://www.ibwfoundation.org.

"Ida B. Wells Monument." Accessed March 7, 2018. http://www.idabwellsmonument.org.

"The Ida B. Wells Society for Investigative Reporting."
  Accessed March 7, 2018. http://idabwellssociety.org.

"Jane Addams – Biographical." Nobelprize.org. Accessed
  March 4, 2018. http://www.nobelprize.org/nobel_prizes/
  peace/laureates/1931/addams-bio.html.

"Jane Addams" in *Feminist Writers*, edited by Pamela Kester-
  Shelton. Detroit, MI: St. James Press, 1996.

Kornblatt, Mark, and Pamela Renner. "'Saint' Jane." *Scholastic
  Update*, February 23, 1990. Academic OneFile. http://link.
  galegroup.com/apps/doc/A8560279/AONE?u=nysl_we_
  becpl&sid=AONE&xid=f4644eb5.

Michaeli, Ethan. *The Defender: How the Legendary Black
  Newspaper Changed America*. New York: Houghton Mifflin
  Harcourt, 2016.

Mintz, Steven, and Sara McNeil. *Digital History*. 2016. http://
  www.digitalhistory.uh.edu.

Rampersad, Arnold. "W. E. B. Du Bois" in *Encyclopedia of
  African-American Culture and History*. Farmington Hills,
  MI: Gale, 2006.

"Reconstruction and Rights." Library of Congress.
  Accessed March 2, 2018. http://www.loc.gov/teachers/
  classroommaterials/presentationsandactivities/
  presentations/timeline/civilwar/recontwo.

Rothenburg, Tamar. "The Long Battle for Women's
  Equality." *Scholastic Update*, May 18, 1987. Academic

OneFile. http://link.galegroup.com/apps/doc/A4839270/
AONE?u=nysl_we_becpl&sid=AONE&xid=c070076f.

"Settlement House Movement" in *Gale Encyclopedia of U.S. Economic History*, 2nd edition, edited by Thomas Riggs, 1187–1190. Vol. 3. Farmington Hills, MI: Gale, 2015.

Sterling, Dorothy. *Black Foremothers: Three Lives*. 2nd edition. New York: The Feminist Press, 1988.

"Susan Brownell Anthony." in *World of Sociology*. Farmington Hills, MI: Gale, 2001.

"Ten Suffragists Arrested While Picketing at the White House." America's Story from America's Library. http://www.americaslibrary.gov/jb/jazz/jb_jazz_sufarrst_1.html.

Washington, Booker T. "Speech to the Atlanta Cotton States and International Exposition. Atlanta, Georgia - September 18, 1895." Accessed March 3, 2018. http://americanradioworks.publicradio.org/features/sayitplain/btwashington.html.

"W. E. B. Du Bois and the NAACP." America's Story from America's Library. Accessed March 5, 2018. http://www.americaslibrary.gov/aa/dubois/aa_dubois_naacp_1.html.

"W. E. B. Du Bois, Growing Up." America's Story from America's Library. Accessed March 5, 2018. http://www.americaslibrary.gov/aa/dubois/aa_dubois_growup_1.html.

Wells-Barnett, Ida B. *On Lynching*. Amherst, NY: Humanity Books, 2002.

Wells, Ida B., Frederick Douglass, Irvine Garland Penn, and
    Ferdinand L. Barnett. *The Reason Why the Colored American
    Is Not in the World's Columbian Exposition.* Urbana, IL:
    University of Illinois Press, 1999.

"Women's Suffrage in the Progressive Era." Library
    of Congress. http://www.loc.gov/teachers/
    classroommaterials/presentationsandactivities/
    presentations/timeline/progress/suffrage.

INDEX

Page numbers in **boldface** refer to images.

ABOUT THE AUTHOR

Naomi E. Jones received her bachelor's of arts degree in history from Brandeis University and her master's of arts degree in history and museum studies from the State University of New York at Buffalo State. As a long time student of history, she particularly enjoys studying women's history and likes to read historical fiction. She currently works for a historic house museum in Western New York.